THE HIGH PRICE OF MONEY

THE HIGH PRICE OF MONEY

An Interpretation of World Interest Rates

PIERLUIGI CIOCCA
and
GIANGIACOMO NARDOZZI

with an essay on

The Main Trends of Real Interest
Rates (1960–1994)

by Aviram Levy and Fabio Panetta

Translated by Timothy Keates

CLARENDON PRESS · OXFORD
1996

Oxford University Press, Walton Street, Oxford OX2 6DP

Oxford New York
Athens Auckland Bangkok Bombay
Calcutta Cape Town Dar es Salaam Delhi
Florence Hong Kong Istanbul Karachi
Kuala Lumpur Madras Madrid Melbourne
Mexico City Nairobi Paris Singapore
Taipei Tokyo Toronto

and associated companies in
Berlin Ibadan

Oxford is a trade mark of Oxford University Press

Published in the United States
by Oxford University Press Inc., New York

Originally published in Italian as
L'alto prezzo del danaro

British Library Cataloguing in Publication Data
Data Available

Library of Congress Cataloging in Publication Data
Ciocca, Pierluigi, 1941–
[Alto prezzo del danaro. English]
The high price of money: an interpretation of world interest
rates / Pierluigi Ciocca and Giangiacomo Nardozzi; with an essay on
The main trends of real interest rates (1960–1994) by Aviram Levy
and Fabio Panetta; translated by Timothy Keates.
Translation of: L'alto prezzo del danaro.
Includes bibliographical references.
1. Interest rates. 2. Economic policy. I. Nardozzi,
Giangiacomo. II. Levy, Aviram. III. Title.
HB539.C5613 1996 332.8'2—dc20 96–12610

ISBN 0–19–828949–9

1 3 5 7 9 10 8 6 4 2

Typeset by BookMan Services, Oxford
Printed in Great Britain
on acid-free paper by
Biddles Ltd., Guildford and King's Lynn

In Memory of Fausto Vicarelli

It is impossible to present a verification of any theory of interest. The facts are too meager, too conflicting, and too intermixed to admit of clear analysis and precise interpretation. In all places and at all times the economic causes tending to make interest high are combined with others tending to make it low. The fact, therefore, that interest is high or low, rising or falling, in conformity with the postulates of a particular theory, does not prove that the theory is the only true explanation. The best that we can expect is to show that the facts as we find them are not inconsistent with the theory maintained.

Irving Fisher, *The Theory of Interest as Determined by Impatience to Spend Income and Opportunity to Invest it* (1930)

PREAMBLE

This book was inspired by our preoccupation with the high price of money that continues to prevail in the world's richest countries. When the book was initially written, in 1992–3, the contrast between the recession in industrial countries—the longest and not among the mildest of the post-war era—and the persistence of high, long-term interest rates was acute. By the time this English edition was completed in the spring of 1995, the countries of the Organization for Economic Cooperation and Development (OECD) had largely come out of the recession. Nonetheless the recovery was accompanied not only by persistently high unemployment but also by a new rise of real interest rates, by almost two percentage points in only one year, 1994. The interest rate hike took place despite the fact that central banks, being reassured by the favourable outlook for inflation, tried to counter it. The high cost of money, which financial markets have once again dictated, persists as a problem for the management of the world economy. The need to understand the causes of the high levels of interest rates from the beginning of the 1980s remains urgent.

Our dissatisfaction with the available explanations led us to retrace the facts, to re-examine their historical background, and to take a fresh look at the theory.

We have felt it necessary to start from a reflection on the ultimate significance of the theory of interest by returning to the foundations laid by Wicksell, Fisher, and Keynes. Our perception of the events is not filtered through econometric exercises intended to corroborate models of interpretation. Rather, we aim to provide the fullest possible picture of the elements that economic theory judges of importance to account for the rate of interest. We have tried to place these elements, pertaining to the last thirty years, in a historical framework, in order to evaluate them with the benefit of a long-term perspective.

Our intent is twofold: to give an account of the significant facts and to persuade of the need to consider the problem of the high cost of money within the paradigm proposed by Keynes. Keynes's approach is centred on the freedom of political action that governments should enlarge and fully utilize, rather than on the necessity of supposedly immutable economic laws: the high rate of interest represents a problem, it can be reduced.

This English edition contains a new chapter (Chapter 7) which deals with the events between 1993 and the beginning of 1995. The tables and graphs relevant to the trends of interest rates have been brought up to date. The events that have occurred after 1993, the year of publication of the book in Italian, do not affect the tendencies which emerge from statistical evidence relative to 1960–92. For the rest, only minor amendments have been made to the Italian text.

Our thanks go to Fabrizio Barca, Anna Carabelli, Paul Corner, Franco Cotula, Stefano Fenoaltea, Giorgio Fodor, Paola Giucca, Timothy Keates, Jan Kregel, Peggy R. Preciado, Sergio Steve, Gianni Toniolo, and Annalisa Verna for their careful reading and the critical comments they provided. Special acknowledgements are due to Eleonora Ciurcina, Mirella Tocci, and Cristina Zago, for their help with the preparation of the typescript. Financial support by the Ministry of the University and Scientific Research is gratefully acknowledged by G. Nardozzi.

P.C.
G.N.

CONTENTS

THE HIGH PRICE OF MONEY

THE MAIN TRENDS OF REAL INTEREST RATES (1960–1994). AN ESSAY BY A. LEVY AND F. PANETTA

THE HIGH PRICE
OF MONEY

Introduction

Between 1988 and 1993 the OECD countries witnessed the
unfolding of a recession which was among the most serious of
the last decades (Table 1). Unlike the stagflations of 1974–5 and
1980–2, the slowdown in productive activity went hand in hand
with low, decreasing inflation. The intensity and rhythm of
the cycle differed markedly among the various economies. In
1993 the economies of continental Europe and Japan went into
full recession, while those of Britain and the United States
began, if somewhat hesitantly, to revive. The (moderate) Anglo-
American expansion spread to continental Europe in 1994. The
Japanese economy continued to stagnate.

The recession arrived at a moment of renewed confidence in
the ability of market forces to promote individual, and hence
collective, well-being. Finance was seen as the most fertile area
in which to reassert and propagate the values of individualism,
and financial systems did indeed undergo a sweeping transformation and development. This same period witnessed the
crisis of the systems promoting rival values: the so-called real
socialism, which collapsed in the Soviet Union and its satellites,
and the non-emerging economies, whose erstwhile champion in
the Islamic world, Iraq, was defeated in the Gulf War.

And yet, these prosperous and successful economies continued to exhibit high interest rates, symptom of scant faith in
the future.

In the countries (United Kingdom, United States, Germany,
France) for which long-term series can most easily be reconstructed,[1] the long-term nominal interest rate at the end of April

---

[1] Over and above the invaluable figures it supplies—which we will make ample use
of in this study—the best reasoned, narrative history dealing with interest rates over a
very long period is still S. Homer, *A History of Interest Rates* (New Brunswick: Rutgers
University Press, 1963), recently re edited by Richard Sylla (3rd edn., New Brunswick:
Rutgers University Press, 1991).

Table 1. Duration and amplitude of the recessions in the industrial countries (1973–1993)[a]

	Index of duration (quarters)		Index of amplitude (output gap[b])		
	Average duration[c]	Duration of last recession[d]	Recession 1973–75	Recession 1979–82	Last recession[d-e]
United States	10	19	0.9	1.1	0.8
Japan	9	8	0.7	0.2	0.4
Germany[f]	9	11	0.9	0.5	0.7
France	11	15	1.0	0.4	0.4
Italy	7	13	1.7	0.3	0.5
United Kingdom	10	20	0.7	0.9	1.0
Canada	8	22	0.5	1.1	1.0

[a] Reference indicator: real gross output. The trend component has been estimated with the Hodrick–Prescott filter. The methodology is described by P. Caselli, 'Fatti stilizzati dell'ultimo ciclo nei principali paesi industrializzati: un confronto con i cicli degli anni Settanta', *Studi e informazioni* (1992), 121–40.

[b] Average quarterly deviation of output from trend, for the periods in which the deviation is negative.

[c] Includes the 1988–93 recession.

[d] Quarters from the preceding peak; the terminal quarter is the final one of 1993; this is assumed to correspond to a trough.

[e] The last recession began in Canada and the United Kingdom in 1988, in Italy and the United States in 1989, in France in 1990, in Japan and Germany in 1991.

[f] Western regions.

Source: ISTAT and OECD data.

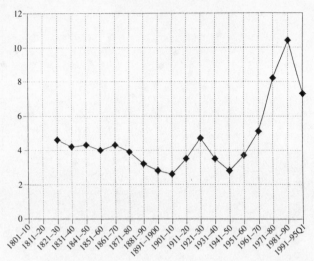

Fig. 1. Long-term nominal interest rates (%), averages for the United States, the United Kingdom, Germany, and France (decadal figures)

Source: see the essay by Levy and Panetta in this volume.

1995 stood at 7.3 per cent, two and a half percentage points above the maximum ten-year averages attained from the early nineteenth century to 1970 (Fig. 1).

In these economies, the average rate of inflation, current and forecasted in the medium term, was below 3 per cent. Hence, the real interest rate—the nominal rate corrected for inflation—was just below the highest average levels—4.5–5 per cent—reached in the two decades of falling prices, 1871–80 and 1931–40 (Fig. 2). Comparing decadal averages, 1981–90 appears noteworthy for real interest rates (5 per cent) that are among the highest achieved historically in times that can be considered normal. This is all the more striking if one accepts the statistical hypothesis of a declining trend in the price of money, world wars and major deflations apart, from the start of the last century to 1970–80.

Over the last twenty years, the mean, long-term real rate in the 'Group of Seven' countries (G-7: United States, United

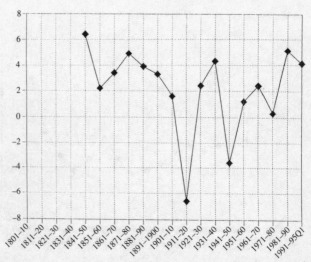

Fig. 2. Long-term real interest rates (%), averages for the United States, the United Kingdom, Germany, and France (decadal figures)
Source: see the essay by Levy and Panetta in this volume.

Kingdom, Italy, Canada, France, Japan, Germany) has fluctuated widely (Fig. 3). This began after the first energy crisis of 1973 with a slide toward negative values, repeated with the second oil crisis at the end of the decade. Real rates then rebounded so strongly as to approach 7 per cent in 1983–4. This level is extraordinarily high, even if it is still well below the single year peaks reached during the deflations of the first half of the nineteenth century and of the 1930s in Germany, the United Kingdom, France and the United States. The return to 'normalcy' following such turbulence has been accompanied by an unusual downward rigidity. The peak attained in the early 1980s was succeeded by persistently high values, with an average of 4.3 per cent for the decade. In contrast, the peaks in the four major countries of 1848 (23 per cent), 1858 (12 per cent), 1878 (12 per cent), 1921 (11 per cent) and 1932 (15 per cent), although well above those of the early 1980s, had been extremely short-lived, reflecting sharp, temporary falls in the prices of goods, especially primary products.

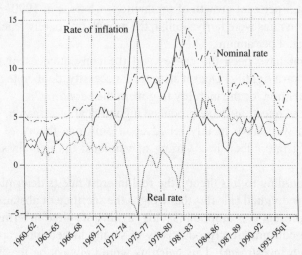

Fig. 3. Long-term nominal interest rate, rate of inflation, and long-term real interest rate in G-7 countries, 1960–1995 (quarterly figures)

Note: the G-7 countries are the United States, the United Kingdom, Canada, Japan, Germany, Italy, and France. The real rate of interest is the nominal rate in the period *t* net of the variation of the average level of prices in the 12 months ending in *t*.

Source: see the essay by Levy and Panetta in this volume.

The interest rates of the individual countries have frequently diverged from the G-7 average. In the 1970s, the long-term real rate was more stable in the United States, more variable in Italy. In the 1970s and 1980s the greatest stability can be found in the German rate throughout the twenty-year period and in the Italian rate in the sub-period 1985–90. Germany was the only country to avoid negative, long-term real rates, even in the 1970s: its lowest figure in the last thirty years, recorded in 1972–3, did not fall below 2.2 per cent.

The G-7 mean, long-term rates were in April 1995 at 7.2 per cent in nominal terms and 4.8 per cent in real terms. Although well below the peaks of 1983–4, the real rate remains more than two percentage points above the trend values of the 1960s. The contrast is underscored by the fact that the industrialized world then experienced, on average, less than 4 per cent inflation and almost 5 per cent growth of production, whereas in 1990–3, if inflation rates were fairly similar, the growth rate barely reached 2 per cent per annum.

What have been the causes and the consequences of this downward rigidity? Does it arise from necessity, deliberate policy intention, or the inability to govern the economy?

These questions have produced a good deal of research. But the answers have mainly relied upon only one theory of the interest rate, albeit in a variety of versions: the neo-classical theory.

According to this theory, the real interest rate is determined by an individual calculus that weighs the sacrifice of abstaining from present consumption (saving) against its yield in terms of future consumption (productivity of saving turned into capital through investment). This calculus would always be feasible, not hindered by uncertainty. The market would express the rationality of individuals by generating a real rate that equates the cost of abstinence, that is of non-consumption, to the yield of invested savings. Economic policy could not avoid taking account of this calculus. For monetary policy, this would involve the credibility of the central banks. Their credibility would be greatest when markets perceive that monetary policy respects the result of markets' calculation (the real rate) and that the institutional autonomy of central banks is devoted to maintaining price stability through rigid policy rules constraining the creation of means of payment.[2] If a central bank abandoned the goal of price stability, which would run counter to its autonomy—understood as the expression of a basic dichotomy

---

[2] In this vein, Milton Friedman's 'monetarist' position is rigorous and consistent, even if debatable in several respects: 'A change in monetary growth affects interest rates in one direction at first but in the opposite direction later on. More rapid monetary growth at first tends to lower interest rates. But later on, the resulting acceleration in spending and still later in inflation produces a rise in the demand for loans, which tends to raise interest rates. In addition, higher inflation widens the difference between real and nominal interest rates. As both lenders and borrowers come to anticipate inflation, lenders demand, and borrowers are willing to offer, higher nominal rates to offset the anticipated inflation. That is why interest rates are highest in countries that *have had* the most rapid growth in the quantity of money and also in prices.' *Money Mischief. Episodes in Monetary History*, (New York: Harcourt Brace Jovanovich, 1992), 49–50.

between money and economic activity—it could reduce the real rate, but only temporarily and with unavoidable inflationary consequences. Government, for its part, can alter the real rate by budgetary manœuvres, but at the cost of a different balance between private and public expenditure. The real rate would thus affect, not the level of income, determined by technology and the labour market, but rather the composition of income, in its sources and uses, and income distribution.

Endorsement of this theory enables one to argue that the level of interest rate is not a problem: it is a fact of 'nature'— unpleasant, perhaps, but unalterable in the short term without cost. One can even make a virtue of necessity and argue that the high price of money represents the proper result of the economic calculus of a society—that of advanced nations—which can presumably make investments with a higher expected real return than in the past, and is willing to make only these investments.[3] Consistent with the neo-classical theory of growth in the version based on exogenous technical progress, the rhythm of growth would not be affected.

Even according to neo-classical theory, it may be doubted whether this natural equilibrium is socially desirable, and whether it should not and could not be altered. But this must be effected through a policy that stimulates saving without interfering with the rationality of the markets. The most widespread opinion blames the high real interest rate on the scarcity of saving and argues that a lower rate can only be achieved through parsimony in public expenditure and incentives to private thrift. This view is echoed in the most recent version of the neo-classical theory of growth, with endogenous technical progress: here, unlike the traditional version, an increased propensity to save has a favourable effect on the growth rate of income.[4]

---

[3] R. J. Barro, 'Pray for High Interest Rates', *Wall Street Journal* (4–5 October 1991); see also 'Savers of the World, Unite', *The Economist* (21 September 1991).

[4] X. Sala i Martin, 'Lecture Notes on Economic Growth. Five Prototype Models of Endogenous Growth', NBER Working Papers (1990), no. 3564. The positive correlation between the propensity to save and the rate of growth in the industrial countries— on which see, among others, C. D. Carroll and L. H. Summers, 'Consumption Growth Parallels Income Growth: Some New Evidence', in B. D. Bernheim and J. B. Shoven

How convincing are these arguments? Are their prescriptions valid? We think not. Our view is that they may actually turn out to be misleading as regards the economic problems the world faces. It is therefore appropriate to put forth again a different, in some sense opposite, vision of capitalism and thus of the rate of interest: the Keynesian vision.

According to Keynes, the intrinsically and peculiarly monetary nature of a capitalist economy and the uncertainty to which it is especially subject render impossible the calculation which underpins the neo-classical equilibrium of the interest rate. The financial markets lack any external point of reference, independent of their behaviour, provided by the 'real' economy. On the contrary, they operate in a regime of 'self-reference' which reflects the judgement of investors and validates it through self-fulfilling expectations. The rationality of financial agents is related to their subjective knowledge and expectations regarding the state of the world and the future as it affects them. It expresses itself through evaluations incorporating *conventional* elements. In Keynes's view, these elements integrate the 'calculus' and the rationalization of surer knowledge: they are 'practical' and simplifying elements, imposed by the need to make decisions, such as custom and inertia, instinct and desire, and prevailing opinion.[5] On such evaluations investors base

(eds.), *National Saving and Economic Performance* (Chicago: University of Chicago Press, 1991)—is attributed to the 'external' economies that may derive from accumulation: in human capital, research and development, specialization in production, international trade, finance, and public infrastructures.

[5] 'The essence of this convention . . . lies in assuming that the existing state of affairs will continue indefinitely, except in so far as we have specific reasons to expect a change . . . We are assuming, in effect, that the existing market valuation, however arrived at, is uniquely *correct* in relation to our existing knowledge of the facts which will influence the yield of the investment, and that it will only change in proportion to changes in this knowledge; though, philosophically speaking, it cannot be uniquely correct, since our existing knowledge does not provide a sufficient basis for a calculated mathematical expectation. In point of fact, all sorts of considerations enter into the market valuation which are in no way relevant to the prospective yield.' J. M. Keynes, *The General Theory of Employment Interest and Money*, (London: Macmillan, 1936), 152. For a critical introduction to the *General Theory*, and to the entire economic thought of Keynes as it developed from *Indian Currency and Finance*, see F. Vicarelli, *Keynes: The Instability of Capitalism* (Philadelphia: University of Pennsylvania Press, 1984). For analysis of the conceptual and semantic problems connected with the

heir decisions in conditions of uncertainty. These evaluations govern the evolution of prevailing opinion and hence the working of financial markets. Market agents rely on these evaluations with a degree of confidence that may vary in time under the influence of uncertainty. Uncertainty, which cannot be eliminated by the economic calculus, is a mutable product of historical time. The interest rate determined—in nominal terms—in the financial market is a matter of convention, not a 'physical' reality. It depends on the level that is considered normal, which makes agents bullish or bearish, and on liquidity preference, related to the degree of confidence in the evaluations.

Economic policy is charged with influencing both the opinion prevailing in the market and the degree of confidence in it. In particular, the central bank acts on the expectations concerning the conventional level of interest. With respect to the market, the effectiveness of its action is determined not by reference to an equilibrium real rate, to be accepted and complied with, but on the ability to persuade markets that is exhibited by the information which is inherent in the direction and modalities of monetary control. This ability depends on the central bank's past record, its reputation and its institutional standing. Even more vitally, it depends on the extent to which the public considers its action 'safe'[6] because it belongs in a coherent and convincing framework of general economic policy and institutional arrangements. In underlining the complementarity among economic policies—monetary, exchange, budgetary, incomes, and structural—Keynes's thought coincides with the rooted conviction of central bankers, including the most orthodox: 'We have never believed that monetary control by itself is a cure-all or a magic incantation, which guarantees success

Keynesian treatment of uncertainty between the *Treatise on Probability* and the *General Theory*, see A. M. Carabelli, *On Keynes's Method* (London: Macmillan, 1988); R. M. O'Donnell, *Keynes: Philosophy, Economics and Politics* (London: Macmillan, 1989); J. A. Kregel, 'Rational Spirits and Postkeynesian Macrotheory of Microeconomics', *De Economist* (1987), 520–532.

6 Keynes, op. cit., 203.

irrespective of what is happening in fiscal policy or on the wage front, or with the exchange rate.'[7]

It is the overall management of the economy that, by orienting market expectations, reducing uncertainty and spreading confidence, can make monetary policy itself effective, especially when this policy is aimed at stimulating economic activity through lower interest rates. It is therefore the evaluation of such management, and not the determination of the real rate of interest, that expresses the rationality of markets: rationality in translating information into the prices of financial instruments, and in setting the nominal rate of interest. The real rate is merely the result obtained from the nominal rate and the rate of inflation. The nominal rate of interest identifies the minimum return required for investment projects considered by the expectations of entrepreneurs operating under uncertainty, moved by 'animal spirits' that generate 'unconscious mental action'.[8] The return required by financial markets is more or less high depending on the convention they assume and the conviction with which the convention is held. Given the expectations of entrepreneurs, the rate of return governs the level of investment and hence that of income. In a monetary economy, this cannot be determined without regard to the financial markets.

These few remarks suggest that Keynes's perspective is based on a concept of history radically different from that which underlies the neo-classical view. The necessity imposed by a calculation that *homo oeconomicus* performs regardless of history is replaced in Keynes by the liberty of *homo faber*. He acts in history and alters its course, through his relationship not so much with nature as with society, groups and other individuals—and also, therefore, by playing a role in economic policy. This is, in our view, a primary reason not to ignore

[7] O. Emminger, 'Postcript', in P. Ciocca (ed.), *Money and the Economy. Central Bankers' Views* (London: Macmillan, 1987), 144.

[8] '*Unconscious mental action*': joining Descartes and almost-Freudian elements Keynes unites in a new concept, harbinger of reflection on the very nature of capitalism, three apparently opposing terms that no other, less brilliant, economist would have dared combine. The quotation, from a manuscript of Keynes's, is in Carabelli, op. cit., 298.

Keynes's vision. The constitution of a new international order following the collapse of the one centred on the confrontation between East and West requires a management of the world economy that can modify and direct the conventions of markets instead of suffering them as constraints.

The second reason not to ignore, indeed, to prefer, Keynes's vision is that the market behaviour postulated by neo-classical theory can be seen as a special case of Keynes's theory. Among the evaluations that make up the opinion of the market there may be room for that based on a sense of a normal real interest rate—and not a nominal one—tied to productivity and thrift, to the point of justifying, to an extreme, a 'monetarist' view of the relation between money, interest, and prices. It is then important to ask oneself—as one cannot in a neo-classical perspective—how this particular evaluation has come to hold sway.[9]

The explanation of high interest rates set forth by monocausal neo-classical theory, centred on the scarcity of saving, leads one to view the economy of the G-7, if not of the entire world, as a single whole. If financial integration justifies, more than in the past, reference to *the* international interest rate, it is nonetheless more difficult to distinguish among specific situations and to underline the relations of interdependence that arise between nations like the United States, Japan and Germany. Different forms, both economic and institutional, characterize the various capitalisms that emerge historically, unlike the single capitalism found in the textbooks. Hence, the third reason for preferring the Keynesian view is the opportunity that it provides to grasp particularities, hierarchies, and dialectics. In managing monetary policy and in singling out the evaluations that actually inspire the financial markets, these factors must not be neglected.

The fourth reason for reappraising Keynes's theory is the danger inherent in the analysis and prescriptions of the neo-classical approach for the growth and stability of the world economy. The view that regards a high real rate of interest as a

---

[9] See G. Nardozzi, 'Joan Robinson and the Rate of Interest these Days', in M. C. Marcuzzo, L. L. Pasinetti, and A. Roncaglia (eds.), *The Economics of Joan Robinson* (London: Routledge, 1996), 81–7.

guarantee of the efficiency of capital underscores the potential for economic and financial crises brought about by the combination of recessionary forces and high interest rates. Those who favour a reduction of real interest rates solely through an increase in the private or public propensity to save assume that such an increase would not interfere with growth in the world economy. They take for granted that a general increase of the propensity to save would lead promptly and reliably to a new path of stable and sustained growth. This is what would happen if investment passively adapted to the level of saving, as the neo-classical theory maintains. But in a monetary economy this need not happen. Faster growth may indeed require a higher propensity to save; but the transition to more rapid growth will not take place if the increase in thrift sets in motion a cumulative process of investment cuts, as entrepreneurs react to the fall in demand. This is clear from the true prototype of modern growth theory, the 'model' of Roy Harrod.[10]

It is difficult, perhaps impossible, and in any case beyond our scope, to adduce conclusive arguments in support of one or the other of the concepts of history that underpin the different theories of interest. Nor do we wish to enter the strictly theoretical debate that continues to oppose Keynes's thought to the neo-classical conception, in its various forms and developments, and also to some versions of the classical one, from the Ricardo of *The High Price of Bullion* to Piero Sraffa and his school.[11] In this introduction we have set forth the basis of our preferences. In the pages that follow we propose to illustrate the reasons why one cannot be satisfied with a neo-classical explanation of the salient facts in the history of interest rates over the last thirty years. Above all, we propose to provide a sense of what can be achieved by a renewed consideration, in

[10] R. F. Harrod, 'An Essay in Dynamic Theory', *Economic Journal* (1939), 14–33, and *Economic Dynamics* (London: Macmillan, 1973).

[11] The reciprocally reinforcing, positive links between Keynes's contribution and Sraffa's critique to the neo-classical theory of interest and capital have been lucidly restated by L. L. Pasinetti, 'The Marginal Efficiency of Investment', in G. C. Harcourt and P. Riach (eds.), *The Second Edition of the General Theory* (London: Routledge, 1996).

light of past events and in view of present problems, of John Maynard Keynes's thought. The room and the means, as well as the opportunity, to shake down a persistently high price of money appear radically different according to whether one moves from a neo-classical, or from a Keynesian, concept of the rate of interest.

1

The Neo-Classical Theory of Interest

According to neo-classical theory,[1] the real interest rate is the price that, in perfect markets capable of ensuring the general equilibrium of the economy, equates desired saving and investment at a level of income that corresponds to full employment. Income is therefore a given, independent as such of the level of investment and of interest rates.

This determination of the interest rate refers to a barter economy. It remains basically unchanged, however, when such an economy is analytically expanded to include a financial system. Money constitutes the means of exchange of a physical product that is itself prior to money and independent of it. Money severs the identity between planned saving (the supply of loans) and investment (the demand for loans). Yet, even in the limiting case of the pure credit economy conceived by Wicksell, money has only a transitory influence on the natural rate of interest, which equilibrates supply and demand in the market for goods. Nor can the rate be altered by the markets. The markets envisioned by Fisher merely add expected inflation to the natural rate of interest. The market for loanable funds generates a nominal rate balancing supply and demand which is equal, with no changes in the price level, to the natural rate that would prevail in an economy without money or credit.

[1] A masterly synthesis of the neo-classical theory of interest and money can be found in D. Patinkin, 'Interest', in *Studies in Monetary Economics* (New York: Harper & Row, 1972). For a fuller treatment see F. Lutz, *The Theory of Interest* (Dordrecht: Reidel, 1967).

Changes in the equilibrium real rate can result from changes in the propensity to save or invest. These variations reflect the forces of thrift and productivity, which alter the natural equilibrium, given the endowments of other factors of production. The different natural rates of interest stemming from the equation of saving and investment represent alternative, and not successive, equilibria. Thrift and productivity signal the impetus for a change in interest rates and not their trend. The latter is derived from the neo-classical theory of growth. It predicts movements in the interest rates which go in an opposite direction to those of the endowment of capital per worker, according to the 'law' of diminishing returns. But these movements ultimately converge towards long-term equilibria in which the interest rate is stable. In equilibrium, both saving and investment grow at a rate equal to the growth of real product, determined by the quantitative and qualitative increase in the labour force. Per capita income and consumption remain constant, as well as the capital : output ratio and, consequently, real interest rates and real wages.

Even in these equilibria, which concern the growth and not the level of income, the interest rate remains insignificant in regard to the overall performance of the economy. It does not enter the determination of long-run growth, just as in the short run it does not determine the aggregate output of goods and services but only its allocation between consumption and investment. Other things being equal, an economy with more saving and a lower interest rate than another will enjoy a higher per capita income, reflecting its greater endowment of capital per worker. However, this will not translate into a more rapid growth in production. The same growth rate is accordingly compatible with a variety of interest rates, even if only that interest rate which is equal to the rate of growth of the labour force, and therefore of the economy, will maximize individual consumption (the 'golden rule' of accumulation).

Money, like real capital, represents wealth. The change in its purchasing power influences consumption (the 'real balance effect' noted by Patinkin). Hence, *stricto sensu*, money does not introduce into the neo-classical theory of interest a new element in addition to thrift and productivity. In the short run the equilibrium real interest rate may be reduced by money creation through open-market purchases by the central bank and by a reduction in the propensity to hold money—as long as money is not entirely 'inside money' (resulting from the bank's intermediation in the borrowing and lending of the private sector alone, which accordingly has no net effect on private wealth) but is at least in part 'outside money' (resulting from State or foreign liabilities, which represent net wealth to the private sector that holds them). The initial excess supply of money then causes a fall in the rate of interest; in a new equilibrium, this is validated by the erosion of private wealth—and therefore by lower consumption—associated with a higher price level. Money created to finance public spending or by a balance of payments surplus instead does not affect the interest rate (neutrality of money): in this case private nominal wealth grows so as to leave unchanged, as the price level increases, private real wealth and consumption.

Neo-classical theory finds a further possible link between money and interest in the redistributive effect of inflation to the extent that it rewards individuals who have a higher propensity to save and constrains those whose income and wealth are penalized to engage in 'forced saving'. The concept of forced saving in economic theory goes back at least as far as Hume and Thornton.[2] It can be broadened to include a variety of processes beyond inflation: as well as inflation, regressive taxation, bank and stock market crises, and the administrative or 'political' manipulation of relative prices and the terms of trade. These processes 'have at least one feature in common, that of representing "abnormal" or "anomalous" redistribution mechanisms, especially when the neoclassical theory of distribution is taken

---

[2] See, in particular, H. Thornton, *An Enquiry into the Nature and Effects of the Paper Credit of Great Britain* (London: Hatchard, 1802), 262–4. The most useful introduction to the concept and its alternating fortunes in the history of economic analysis is still that of F. Machlup, 'Forced or Induced Saving: An Exploration into its Synonyms and Homonyms', *Review of Economics and Statistics* (1943), 26–39.

as the "norm".[3] However, from the standpoint of the neo-classical theory of interest under consideration here, what matters is the sequence: money creation, forced saving, lower interest rate.[4]

Analogous to the hypotheses of forced saving, by their equally *ad hoc* nature, are the hypotheses of price rigidity and unemployment. In this case, the impulse deriving from increased supply of or reduced demand for money lowers the interest rate in the short term, when this rigidity is in operation. In particular, the model known as IS–LM, which incorporates traits of Keynesian analysis in a 'neo-classical synthesis',[5] differs from the strictly neo-classical model in admitting non-natural equilibria resulting from variations in the quantities produced and not in the prices. It retains the reference to the natural equilibrium at full employment towards which the economy is said to tend when wages and prices are flexible, and towards which economy policy should be directed since, among other things, it is unable to determine permanent deviations from equilibrium. Nevertheless, even if the forces of thrift and productivity prevail in the long run, in the short run the changes in the equilibrium interest rate can be determined without regard

[3] P. Ciocca, 'Formazione dell'Italia industriale e «storia econometrica»', *Rivista Internazionale di Scienze Sociali* (1969), 550.

[4] 'The essence of this doctrine is that an exogenous increase in the quantity of money which accrues initially to entrepreneurs, or those who lend to them, will increase the proportion of an economy's expenditures going into investment, and that the necessary corresponding increase in savings will be forced upon workers and fixed-income recipients by the inflationary price movement which the monetary expansion generates. In this way such an expansion can increase the amount of real capital in the economy. But if it can do this, it can also lower the marginal productivity of capital and thereby the long-run equilibrium rate of interest.' D. Patinkin, *Money, Interest and Prices* (2nd edn., New York: Harper & Row, 1965), 371. The harshest criticism of the use that neo-classical business cycle theory makes of the notion of forced saving is that of Piero Sraffa, in the debate with Hayek published in the *Economic Journal* of 1932. At a meeting at Turin's Fondazione Einaudi, in March 1967, Sraffa told one of the authors of the present work that he had no objection to the concept as such- even in the broad sense- nor to its cautious application in the historical analysis of inflationary processes, or episodes of banking and financial instability.

[5] See the original version of J. R. Hicks, 'Mr Keynes and the Classics', *Econometrica* (1937), 147–59, together with Hicks's 'self criticism' published forty years later, 'IS–LM: An Explanation', *Journal of Post-Keynesian Economics* (Winter 1980–1), 139–54.

to the stringent hypothesis of full employment. These changes can also occur in the wake of variations in spending that call forth changes in supply and in saving through linkages that recall the Keynesian mechanism. *Ceteris paribus*, economic policy influences the real rate, altering it in the opposite direction to the supply of money and in the same direction as the public deficit. The intensity of these effects depends on the value of the parameters that determine the slope of the IS–LM curves and of the Phillips curve.

In the long run, according to the neo-classical models of growth with money,[6] a more rapid expansion of the money stock implies an acceleration of the inflationary process. The lower return on money held as wealth, eroded by higher inflation, reduces the demand for it and increases the demand for real capital, given the propensity to save. The faster accumulation of real capital implies a decline in the equilibrium real rate, which matches the resulting decline in the productivity of capital. This yields the inverse relation between the rate of inflation and the real rate of interest observed by Fisher. But this is not a disequilibrium resulting from an inadequate adjustment of expectations in financial markets; rather, there are new, natural, long-run equilibria.

Beyond new equilibrium values, in the neo-classical scheme changes in the interest rate can also reflect deviations from equilibrium associated with a surplus or a shortage of saving with respect to investment. Here factors other than thrift and productivity come into play. The adjustment toward another equilibrium is then promoted by economic policies and expectations. In the mechanism Wicksell envisaged, if the banking system—central bank included—employs an interest rate that differs from the natural one, the ensuing variations in prices affect the supply of credit and bring the interest rate back to its equilibrium level. Wicksell emphasizes the inconstancy of the forces that determine 'the normal or natural real rate': 'It is

[6] J. Tobin, 'Money and Economic Growth', *Econometrica* (1965), 671–84; D. Levhari and D. Patinkin, 'The Role of Money in a Simple Growth Model', *American Economic Review* (1968), 713–53.

essentially variable'.[7] He therefore also highlights the role of monetary and banking policy as determinants of the bank rate (the market rate) during the frequent changes in the natural equilibrium: this is the cause of 'the trade cycles and economic crises'.[8] According to Fisher, the real rate is heir to slower movements over time: 'The causes making for high or low interest rates tend to counteract themselves'.[9] Impatience can vary widely among individuals and societies, but in both it represents something almost innate and therefore it tends to be stable. The 'opportunity to invest' depends mainly on technical progress, whose effect, however, 'is confined to the period of exploitation of the new invention, and is succeeded later by an opposite tendency'.[10] Shorter-run variations in real rates stem mainly from belated adjustments of expectations to the rate of inflation, which is governed by monetary policy and poorly perceived by financial markets. Perfect financial markets would set the nominal rate by adding to a stable equilibrium real rate the rate of inflation correctly anticipated over the terms of the loans (the 'Fisher effect').[11]

If the movement of the real interest rate reflects a new equilibrium, a higher real rate will obtain, not with an excess of investment over saving, but with a higher expected yield on capital and/or a stronger preference for present consumption out of full employment income. If its movements instead reflect disequilibrium processes, a higher rate can result from a variety

[7] K. Wicksell, *Lectures on Political Economy* (London: Routledge & Sons, 1946 (1906), vol. ii), 193. Among the causes that reduce the natural rate, Wicksell notes, along with greater saving, 'increasing prosperity, increased legal security, increased forethought and a higher level of civilization . . . Conversely, the rate of interest rises when the amount of capital diminishes, either relatively, for example, through an increase in population and the resulting increased demand for capital in excess of current savings, or absolutely, as the result of a destructive war or some catastrophe of nature. But the rate of interest may also rise for a time in consequence of some technical discovery which opens up a hitherto unknown profitable employment for capital and which at the same time usually requires more capital for its realization' (205–6).

[8] Ibid., 209–14.

[9] I. Fisher, *The Theory of Interest as Determined by Impatience to Spend Income and Opportunity to Invest it* (New York: Kelley & Macmillan, 1954 (1930)), 372.

[10] Ibid., 502.

[11] I. Fisher, *Appreciation and Interest*, American Economic Association Monographs, III series, vol. 11, no. 4, American Economic Association, (London: Macmillan, 1896).

of situations. It may represent a recovery from a Wicksellian disequilibrium, in which the rate determined by monetary policy is less than the natural rate and the investment exceeds saving; in this case, the increase in the rate of interest is accompanied by a reduction of the excess of investment over saving. On the other hand, it may represent the start of a Fisherian disequilibrium, if a decline of the rate of inflation is poorly perceived by the financial markets; in this case the increase in the rate of interest is accompanied by a growing excess of saving. In neither of the two cases, therefore, is the rise in real interest rate associated with a greater excess of investment over saving.

2

Neo-Classical Theory and the Facts

Neo-classical theory predicts definite associations between specific quantitative variables and the level of the interest rate. In its fundamental design, the theory aims to be tested empirically, even statistically and econometrically. Yet in moving beyond the hypotheses to confront the facts, one encounters in the first place a serious data problem. The variables cannot be directly observed. The interest rate, the saving, and the investment that are recorded in the statistics are not those on which economic agents are supposed to base plans and decisions to save and to invest: rather, they are the actual ones, which normally have not been determined in the condition of full employment postulated by the theory. The real interest rate observed is the nominal rate corrected for changes in the price level, not the 'pure' rate, strictly at constant prices, contemplated by the theory. It may be approximated by the yield of capital revealed by the earnings of firms or investment in their financial liabilities. But this is still an *ex post* value, not the one underlying decisions. The saving and investment of the national income accounts do not necessarily correspond to a neo-classical equilibrium if they are equal, nor to a disequilibrium if they differ.

This should be borne in mind in assessing the validity of the empirical verification of the theory, notably in its Wicksellian and Fisherian versions. There is a problem of consistency between empirical observation and the logical structure of the theory as well as a problem of correspondence between the observed variables and those referred to by the theory.

Both problems are confronted in the empirical studies[1] on the trends of real interest rates, saving, and investment. The data show a growing share of saving and investment in national income for the OECD economies up to the early 1970s; a drastic fall with the crisis of 1975, and a renewed decline, after a recovery at the end of the decade, in the 1980s. Moreover, the OECD economies passed from an overall excess of saving over investment (current account surplus) in the 1960s to an overall saving deficit in the 1980s. As a matter of method, the mere observation of these time paths, even if still *ex post* and with a highly variable rate of unemployment, should discourage one from correlating them with the interest rate in the neo-classical framework. The variability to be found in the shares of income saved and invested suggests that the system evolved by shifting from one equilibrium to another: the outcome is uncertain, since in disequilibrium the path of the rate of interest is governed by forces other than thrift and productivity. The deterioration of the current account balance between the 1960s and the 1980s could only mean that the rate of interest was higher in the earlier period and lower in the later period than the level consistent with equilibrium in the balance of payments with the rest of the world.

Among the econometric studies that consider the path of the real interest rates in 1960–90 as a succession of natural equilibria, that by Barro and Sala i Martin deserves attention.[2] The model is Wicksellian in its design, as the equations estimate the (short-term) real rate for the economies of the 'Group of 10' countries (G-7, Sweden, Belgium and The Netherlands, plus Switzerland) through reduced forms obtained by equating investment and desired savings out of income. The model is eclectic in its construction, however, as the saving function includes, among its arguments, the price of oil (as a proxy for transitory

[1] See, for instance, A. Dean *et al.*, 'Saving Trends and Behaviour in OECD Countries', OECD Economic Studies (1990), no. 14, 7–58.
[2] R. J. Barro and X. Sala i Martin, 'World Real Interest Rates', NBER Working Papers (1990), no. 3317, and R. J. Barro, 'World Interest Rates and Investment', NBER Working Papers (1991), no. 3849.

income), the growth in the money stock, and the path of budget deficits. The study concludes that, for the aggregate of the industrialized market economies, real interest rates are explained by oil prices, stock market returns (a proxy for the expected return to capital) and, to a lesser extent, monetary policy. Intercountry differences in real rates are not explained by country-specific factors, including notably the return to capital and monetary policies. The use of income-related saving and investment functions is consistent with the neo-classical hypothesis that income is determined by supply conditions and therefore independent of the level of saving and investment. But one should then presume the following: (i) that the real rates observed and explained by the model are always the natural rates; (ii) that the transition from one equilibrium to another is instantaneous (a hypothesis rejected by Wicksell); and, (iii) that the G-10 economy has remained at full employment over the thirty-year period. The eclecticism of the model does not warrant this Wicksellian interpretation. The presence of the money stock and of the budget deficit among the arguments of the saving function means that the actual real rates cannot correspond to natural equilibria. They appear rather to belong to a Keynesian context, in which the level of income is influenced by monetary and fiscal policy. One must therefore give up the hypothesis of full employment. With it, the logical basis for relating saving and investment to income weakens, as the latter is no longer predetermined by supply. The econometric results do not seem supported by a rigorous theoretical framework. The conclusions concerning the determinants of the movements of the world interest rate appear ambiguous.

The link between the price of oil and the real rate of interest is treated also as a matter of forced saving by Bruno and Sachs, in what is perhaps the most thorough analysis of the crisis of the 1970s from a neo-classical perspective. Bruno and Sachs start from the observation that 'aggregate world consumption falls with an increase in the real price of oil if the marginal propensity to consume of the net oil exporter(s) is less than the weighted marginal propensity to consume of the net importers'.[3] In their view, the low real interest rates of 1974–7 are attributable not only to the decline in profits and investment in the industrial economies that followed the oil price hike of 1973–4, but also to a transitory rise in saving in the OPEC countries. The latter supposedly 'more than compensated',[4] on a world level, the decline in saving in the OECD area. After the second oil crisis, it is suggested, there was instead a smaller decline in the OECD countries' investment, while world saving may have been reduced not only by a greater decline in the industrialized area (large budget deficits) but also by a smaller increase in the OPEC area: from 1974 to 1979 the OPEC economies would have had the time to develop their spending capacity. The *ad hoc* character of the neo-classical hypothesis of forced saving is evident. It is implausible that the OPEC countries' *ex ante* urge to spend was not already very strong at the time of the first oil crisis, when their economies were often very poor and beset by urgent structural problems. If one considers the *ex post* data now available (Table 2), the OPEC area's saving rate did indeed decline between the middle 1970s and the end of the 1980s, from 40 per cent to one fifth of GDP. But in 1980–4, after the second oil crisis, it remained well above the saving rate of the industrial countries, with a gap (25 versus 21 per cent) much lower than that of 1975–9 (40 versus 23 per cent), after the first oil crisis: a sufficient gap, in any case, to derive an increase in world saving from the redistributive effects of the second oil crisis as well as the first. The gap between the two areas' *ex post* propensity to save became negative in 1985–6, but the sharp fall in oil prices of 1986 does not seem to have had the effect—which according to the argument of Bruno and Sachs it should have helped bring about—of increasing world saving and so reducing the real rate of interest.

Reconsidered in the light of the IS–LM model, the actual path of the real rate comes to depend both on the parameters of the IS–LM and Phillips curves and on the combination of impulses and economic policies that reality, in which things are not held

---

[3] M. Bruno and J. Sachs, *Economics of Worldwide Stagflation*, (Oxford: Blackwell, 1985), 82.   [4] Ibid., 83.

Table 2. Saving in the OECD and OPEC areas and in the World (as percentage of output)

	Industrial countries	Oil-producing countries[a]	World	Ratio of GNP of OPEC to world GNP[b]
1975–9	23.2	40.7	24.7	4.7
1980–4	21.3	25.2	22.6	5.3
1985	20.8	19.5	22.5	5.1
1986	20.5	16.4	22.3	
1987	20.6	19.0	23.3	
1988	21.4	16.5	23.5	
1989	21.6	19.1	23.8	
1990	20.9	23.3	23.5	2.5
1991	20.6	20.6	22.6	
1992	19.6	20.1	21.9	
1993	19.3	17.0	21.9	2.7
1994	19.9	21.2	23.1	
1995	20.0	21.3	23.6	

[a] Group of 19 countries (more or less identical with OPEC) exporting mainly energy products according to the classification of the IMF.
[b] Percentage points; in 1970–4 the average ratio was 2.4 per cent.

Sources: IMF, *World Economic Outlook* (October 1995); World Bank, *Annual Development Report* (various issues).

constant, always brings about. This eclectic model of interest rate movements does little more than refer back to the forces of productivity and thrift in a long period that remains to be defined. It underscores the interest rate's sensitivity, reflected in parameters to be estimated econometrically, to economic policy and exogenous influences on inflationary expectations, and to supply and demand. Not surprisingly, therefore, empirical tests based on the IS–LM model rarely yield conclusive results. They reveal significant inverse correlations between real interest and inflation rates (the Mundell–Tobin effect) both in the short run (United Kingdom and United States) and in the long run (United States). But they also reveal significant determinants of the real rate that are independent of inflationary expectations, confirming the model's predictions about the effectiveness of economic

Table 3. G-7 countries: real interest rates; rate of saving and investment; capital intensity and productivity; rate of growth of money and output.

	1960–9	1970–9	1980–9
Real interest rates			
short term	1.7	−0.8	3.4[a]
long term	2.3	0.2	4.3[a]
Rate of saving[b]	23.5	23.2	21.1
Rate of investment[b]	21.8	22.5	21.3
Current account balance[b]	0.5	0.3	−0.4
Rate of profit[c]	23.8[d]	17.3	13.8
Real gross capital stock per employee (whole economy) index, 1985 = 100	72.2 (1970)	89.7 (1980)	109.1 (1989)

		1970–9		1980–9	
Average rates of growth of money stock (M3) and gross output		nominal	real	nominal	real
money[e]		11.1	4.2	7.8	2.7
output[e]		10.5	3.0	7.3	2.2

[a] Average 1980–92.
[b] The ratios are expressed as percentage of output.
[c] Ratio of gross operating margin to gross capital stock in manufacturing industry.
[d] France and Italy are not included.
[e] For the decade 1970–9 the growth rates start from 1972.

Sources: BIS, IMF and OECD (national accounts) and the essay by Levy and Panetta in this volume.

policy. Nevertheless, the econometric attempts to measure the effects of monetary and fiscal policy on long-term interest rates do not allow one to draw sufficiently robust conclusions.[5]

The neo-classical approach is heir to problems which do not emerge only from a critical examination of the literature. They are confirmed by the poor correspondence between the basic propositions of the theory concerning interest rates and the main stylized facts of the industrial economies over the past three decades.

There is no evidence (Table 3) that the high real interest rate of the 1980s stemmed from a non-transitory change in the preceding equilibria brought about by changes in parsimony and productivity. The movements of the so-called fundamental forces do not appear to have been consistent in direction, extent, and timing with a neo-classical interpretation of real interest rates that swung dramatically over a few years from negative to historically high positive values. The fact that between the 1960s and the 1980s in the industrial countries the propensity to save fell more than the propensity to invest can lend itself to an exercise in comparative statics. In picturing the two situations one can attribute the higher real rates of the 1980s to an upward shift of the savings schedule greater than the downward shift in the investment schedule. Nonetheless, the decline in the saving : income ratio was only marginally greater than the decline in the investment : income ratio. Over twenty years, the deterioration of the G-7 area's balance on current account—apart from the so-called errors and omissions which affect the data—does not even reach 1 per cent of output. *Ex post* data may reflect feedbacks from the path of the interest rates themselves, especially in the case of investment. Above all, the new and higher equilibrium interest rate in the 1980s should have coincided with a higher return to capital, and a lower capital

[5] For a survey see C. J. Green, 'The Determination of Interest Rates and Asset Prices: A Survey of Theory and Evidence', in C. J. Green and D. T. Llewellyn (eds.), *Surveys in Monetary Economics*, vol. i (*Monetary Theory and Policy*) (Oxford: Blackwell, 1991), 74–149. See also M. D. Levi and J. H. Makin, 'Anticipated Inflation and Interest Rates: Further Interpretation of Findings on the Fisher Equation', *American Economic Review* (1978), 801–12.

intensity, than in the 1960s and 1970s. But this is in no way supported by the figures. In industry, at least, the decadal average gross profit rate is noticeably lower in the 1980s than in the 1960s, and in the 1970s. The capital : labour ratio kept growing in the 1980s, at a rate (22 per cent over the decade) only marginally below that of the 1970s (24 per cent). These results obtain for each of the G-7 countries as well as for their aggregate.

As to the modes and intensity of technical progress, so frequently and variously invoked by neo-classical explanations of interest rates,[6] the 1970s—with low or negative real rates—and the 1980s—with positive and high real rates—appear in the main more similar than different.

Albeit very cautiously, studies of technical progress tend to place a dividing line 'in 1973'. They contrast the period 1970–90 as a whole with the period 1950–70. In 1973–9 and 1979–88 labour and total productivity growth were very similar and very mild, equivalent to about one third of those of 1950–73, which were exceptionally high even in historical perspective. The productivity of capital continued along its declining trend, at an average rate that over the entire period 1973–88 turned out to be more than twice that of 1960–73; in the sub-period 1979–88 the decline (–0.8 per cent per year) was slower than in the preceding sub-period 1973–79 (–1.5 per cent).[7] What remains unresolved, analytically, is the contradiction—'Solow's paradox'—between the intuitive sense of important variations in the rate of technical progress between 1973 and the end of the 1980s and the lack of evidence of such variations in the path of total factor productivity. Among those scholars who pursued a historical, qualitative and sectoral approach some at least are convinced that one can speak of an 'industrial divide'. But they see it as getting under way, as noted, 'in 1973', in the wake of the changes in the

---

[6] 'The interplay of impatience and opportunity on the rate of interest is profoundly influenced by invention and discovery. The range of man's investment opportunity widens as his knowledge extends and his utilization of the forces and materials of Nature grows. With each advance in knowledge come new opportunities to invest. The rate of return over cost rises.' Fisher, *The Theory of Interest*, 341.

[7] OECD, *Technology/Economy Programme (TEP)*. Draft Background Report, (Paris, 1990), ch. 1.

relative prices of labour and primary products worldwide. This technological watershed may prove as epochal as that which marked 'the early nineteenth-century victory of mass production over craft production as the dominant form of industrial organization'.[8] And yet these scholars remain perplexed as to the exact nature of the new course and the speed and modalities of its unfolding over the 1970s and the 1980s.[9] More recent attempts to ascribe the empirical features of technical progress to general categories, though very uncertain, do not seem to find sharp lines of demarcation between the 1970s and the 1980s.[10]

There is no evidence to confirm the further hypothesis that the high, real interest rate of the 1980s resulted from a non-transitory change in previous equilibria attributable to changes in money supply or demand. Problems arise even if one starts from two basic assumptions about the 1980s: that of a systematic and continuous restriction of the supply of money, carried out by central banks through open-market sales of government bonds, and/or that of a structural, and perhaps accelerated, increase in the income elasticity of the demand for money. In fact, though there was an overall tendency towards restriction, in the 1980s the monetary policies of the main countries differed in their orientation and implementation. Again in the 1980s, there is no statistical evidence of an increase in the transactions demand for money.[11] As to the wealth effect hypothesized by

[8] M. J. Piore and C. F. Sabel, *The Second Industrial Divide. Possibilities for Prosperity* (New York: Basic Books, 1984), 15.

[9] This may turn out to be 'a period of confused experimentation in which society discovered how to make economic use of efficiency advances in mass production', or instead 'a time when industrial society returned to craft methods of production', ibid., 251–2.

[10] G. Dosi, 'Sources, Procedures and Microeconomic Effects of Innovation', *Journal of Economic Literature* (1988), 1120–71.

[11] The empirical analyses of the past few years have shown that when the functional dynamics are properly specified and the process of financial innovation is properly allowed for, the demand for money in the major industrial countries remained stable over the 1970s and 1980s. The exception is Italy, where the demand for money was primarily financial in the 1970s and transaction-related in the 1980s. See D. F. Hendry and N. R. Ericsson, 'Modelling the Demand for Narrow Money in the United Kingdom and the United States', *European Economic Review* (1991), 833–86; J. M. Boughton, 'Long-Run Money Demand in Large Industrial Countries', IMF Staff Papers (1991), 1–32; K. Cuthbertson, 'Modelling the Demand for Money', in C. J. Green and D. T.

neo-classical monetary theory, it must be pointed out that the 1980s were also a period of inflation, albeit at reduced rates; moreover, in the main industrial countries government debt, even though increasing with respect to income, barely exceeds 10 per cent of aggregate gross financial assets. Neither condition can have favoured a higher cost of money by cutting saving through a 'real balance' effect: an effect that even those who propound it admit 'empirically has been shown to be fairly weak'.[12] With reference to the neo-classical models of equilibrium growth with money, one notes that the expansion of the money supply, far from lagging behind or slowing down with respect to the growth of real product so as to exert upward pressure on the real rate of interest, exceeded real product growth, by a margin comparable to that of the 1970s (Table 3).

Finally, there is no evidence that the high real interest rate of the 1980s was part of a Fisherian or Wicksellian disequilibrium.

As noted, the Fisherian version of neo-classical theory predicts that the real interest rate remains constant while the variations of the nominal rate reflect those of expected inflation. Empirically, this prediction has found support neither in Fisher's own observations, nor in the majority of subsequent studies. This is true even of the most recent studies, notwithstanding Fama's ingenious attempt to rehabilitate Fisher's theory by showing that the difference between nominal rates and a constant real rate is a good indicator of expected inflation, as predicted by the theory of efficient markets.[13]

The correlations presented in this book do not favour the

Llewellyn (eds.), op. cit.; C. Monticelli and M. O. Strauss-Kahn, 'Broad Monetary Aggregates and National Money Demand in Europe', *Economie et Société* (1992), 147–97.

[12] Patinkin, *Interest*, 138. Only in Canada (12.6 per cent) and above all in Italy (23.5 per cent) did the liabilities of the public sector exceed 10 per cent of aggregate gross financial assets (December 1991).

[13] J. Carmichael and P. W. Stebbing, 'Fisher's Paradox and the Theory of Interest', *American Economic Review* (1983), 619–30; L. H. Summers, 'The Non-adjustment of Nominal Interest Rates: A Study of the Fisher Effect', in *Macroeconomics, Prices and Quantities. Essays in Memory of Arthur M. Okun* (Oxford: Blackwell, 1983), 201–44; E. F. Fama, 'Short-Term Interest Rates as Predictors of Inflation', *American Economic Review* (1975), 269–82; R. Rovelli, 'Expected Inflation and the Real Interest Rate: A Survey of Current Issues', *Giornale degli Economisti* (1984), 671–97.

'Fisher effect'; rather, they confirm the variability of the real interest rate *vis-à-vis* higher (the 1970s) or lower (the 1980s) inflation. This variability does not appear to represent deviations from Fisherian equilibrium. On the basis of *ex post* data the drastic fall in the real rates in the 1970s does not appear to have been accompanied by the excess of investment over saving contemplated by Fisherian disequilibrium. The subsequent rise in rates does not appear to have been accompanied by the opposite excess of saving over investment. The fall in the real rate in the 1970s was accompanied by an acceleration of inflation and its rise in the 1980s by a deceleration. But the declining inflation in the second half of the 1980s was not coincident with the rise in the real rate of interest. The recovery of profitability, in the same period, contradicts the hypothesis of a constant real rate of interest.

An interpretation based on Wicksellian disequilibria seems similarly to be rejected. Had the particularly low real rate of the 1970s been due to monetary policies that were excessively expansionary with respect to the natural rate, more rapid inflation should then have been accompanied by an excess of investment, of which there is no sign in those years of stagflation. Moreover, the recovery from this supposed disequilibrium should also have involved a rise in the interest rate until it stabilized at its natural rate, and not the rise and subsequent fall actually observed over the 1980s. This last occurrence was not in fact accompanied either by an increase in profitability (evidence of a rise in the natural interest rate) in the early 1980s, nor by a subsequent decline (similarly evidence of a fall in the natural rate): to the contrary, profitability was lowest in the early 1980s and rising from 1983 and 1988.

3

The Keynesian Approach

What distinguishes Keynes's thought from neo-classical thought is the idea that market rationality manifests itself through conventions rather than models of reality that are held to be true according to positivist canons.

A convention is a rule defined by a rationality that reflects not the truth of a theory but the convenience of consciously relying on it in order to act, in accordance with a practical philosophy in a world that is imperfectly known.[1] Keynes employs different terms to distinguish between the element of calculation and the element of convention. He sees the second of these as almost inescapably linked with the first. To emphasize its importance, we shall here use the term convention in a broader sense, to mean the valuation made by individuals, and ultimately prevailing in the market, rationally determined not only by reliance on schemes for explaining phenomena, but also by elements that are crucial to action and cannot be considered as part of these schemes (since, as Keynes points out, they are 'in no way relevant to the prospective yield').

Unlike positivist rationality, which is motivated by what is true or false, Keynes's practical rationality considers whether something is convenient or not. It varies therefore with the circumstances in which one is to act—circumstances contingent upon events or history. Rather than temporary or inconstant, the conventional elements that in Keynes's view necessarily enter evaluations and market decisions are characteristically uncertain,

---

[1] Carabelli, op. cit., especially chs. 3 and 9 and pp. 300–1. For a partly different view of conventions in the evolution of Keynes's thought, see T. Lawson, 'Keynes and Conventions', *Review of Social Economics* (1993), no. 2, 174–200.

and not the fruit of certain knowledge or unequivocally as-sociated with 'physical' phenomena or 'objective' facts. The influence exerted by an event, through expectations, on the pre-vailing opinion of market agents—optimists and pessimists—depends on the context. It is the task of economic analysis to identify such influences as they occur; that is, to go beyond the notion of 'however arrived at' and to reconstruct the ways in which the 'existing market evaluation' comes to exist.

Keynes understands interest as a conventional phenomenon, determined by a variety of possible types of behaviour. His theory is not based on the typical neo-classical economic agent, deemed rational because it strives to grasp the 'fundamental' causes of the interest rate identified by theory, albeit in its vari-ous versions (Fisherian, Wicksellian, IS–LM). Keynes asserts that the 'actual value' of the interest rate 'is largely governed by the prevailing view as to what its value is expected to be. Any level of interest which is accepted with sufficient conviction as *likely* to be durable *will* be durable'.[2] His assertion expresses a theory which provides for a variety of conventional modes of behaviour to determine the level of interest. Robertson over-looked the analytical advantage derived from the multiplicity of the elements that may enter a convention: 'Thus the rate of interest is what it is because it is expected to become other than it is, there is nothing left to tell us why it is what it is. The organ which secretes it has been amputated, and yet it somehow still exists—a grin without a cat.'[3] In a similar vein, Hicks asserted that Keynesian theory would leave interest 'hanging by its own bootstraps'.[4] Both viewpoints imply that conventions are based

---

[2] Keynes, op. cit., 203.

[3] D. H. Robertson, *Essays in Monetary Theory* (London: Staples Press, 1946 (1940)), 25.

[4] 'We have already seen, in our earlier chapter on interest, that a part of the interest paid on actual securities is to be attributed to default risk; and a part of the interest paid, at least on long-term securities, is to be attributed to uncertainty of the future course of interest rates. Both of these elements are purely risk-elements; if these were the only elements in interest, it would be true to say that all interest is, in the end, nothing but a risk-premium. That is, I take it, the view of Mr Keynes; his doctrine of "Liquidity Preference" appears to reduce all interest into terms of these two risk factors. But to say that the rate of interest on perfectly safe securities is determined by nothing else but uncertainty of future interest rates seems to leave interest hanging by its own bootstraps;

on propositions that are true or false rather than convenient or inconvenient; consequently they would impose the acceptance of a single model of behaviour because it is 'true'. But individuals select specific models of behaviour from a range of possibilities that reflect their 'beliefs' and their 'degree of confidence' in them.

This means that different conventional models can be hypothesized, depending on the specific historical circumstances to which the analysis applies. In fact, according to Keynes, the probability financial market operators assign to a proposition, e.g. that the bond rate will be higher one month ahead, depends on the amount of relevant favourable knowledge compared with unfavourable knowledge. The choice between relevant knowledge (relevant evidence or simply relevant arguments) and irrelevant knowledge is based on a judgement that is essentially intuitive and hence linked to particular circumstances. Thus, in certain circumstances, the knowledge that is relevant for believing the interest rate will be higher within one month may be merely information on the rate of inflation; in other circumstances, it may be the expected outcome of a G-7 summit meeting. In yet other circumstances, the expectation that the interest rate will rise may be based on the factors likely to induce the central bank to send a signal to the government by raising short-term rates. The convention might also be based on 'real' aspects of the economy. This occurs, as Keynes himself noted,[5] when the market looks to the level of interest corresponding to full employment or, as indicated by Joan Robinson, whenever 'the real forces play some part in shaping . . . the historical experience of interest rates which the community has lived through'.[6] In this last instance, productivity and thrift may

one feels an obstinate conviction that there must be more in it than that.' J. R. Hicks, *Value and Capital. An Inquiry into Some Fundamental Principles of Economic Theory* (2nd edn., Oxford: Clarendon Press, 1946), 163–4.

[5] Keynes, op. cit., 202. For Keynes, obviously, in a monetary economy nothing is more objective and important, and in this sense 'real', than expectations: 'A monetary economy . . . is essentially one in which changing views about the future are capable of influencing the quantity of employment and not merely its direction' (ibid., p. vii).

[6] J. Robinson, 'The Rate of Interest', in *Collected Economic Papers*, vol. ii (Oxford: Blackwell, 1964), 247.

also take their place in a Keynesian determination of the rate of interest, but always as expectations, or as temporary and in-constant conventions. At times there may be several reasonable propositions whose probabilities cannot be compared because they are based on different arguments. For example, there may be two opposite propositions concerning the future level of interest rates. One may be based on reasons regarding the economy, which is perceived to be incapable of bearing higher rates; the other may be based on the central bank's unwilling-ness to deviate from its previously announced money supply targets. In such cases, there is uncertainty that can only be resolved by seeking new evidence that will increase the weight of the argument, either by relying on instinct and imitation or else by abstaining from decision and action.[7] The choice of the convention to direct the analysis is thus to be determined on a practical level.[8]

The liquidity preference curve expresses this theory without identifying a single conventional model, assumed to be relevant in each circumstance. Along the curve one finds all the possible values of the nominal long-term interest rate, consistent with equilibrium in the market for the existing stock of bonds with

[7] For an application of this approach to the New York Stock Exchange see G. Nardozzi, 'Il mercato interpreta la propria volatilità: evidenze dalla borsa di New York (1976–1992) utili per un miglior dialogo fra economisti e operatori', *IRS, Rapporto sul mercato azionario*, (Milan: Il Sole 24 Ore Libri, 1995).

[8] In his latest comparison between Keynes and the classics Hicks says: 'A model in which all these things were taken into account could not, I think, have failed of acceptance, at least in principle, both by Robertson and by Keynes. But, having got so far in agreement, they would still have had their differences. These would not have been theoretical differences, in a narrow sense; they would have been differences of judgment on which of the choice margins that had been identified were of practical importance. This, being an empirical question, could have been answered, quite properly, in different ways at different times . . . To deal at all adequately with the historical questions which thus come into sight would require research.' J. R. Hicks, *A Market Theory of Money* (Oxford: Clarendon Press, 1989), 75. Here Hicks seems to relinquish the methodological device of unequivocally deducing 'the changes in expectations from the changes in the objective data by which they are provoked'. The original intention of the method stated by Hicks in *A Suggestion for Simplifying the Theory of Money* is criticized by J.A. Kregel, 'Conceptions of Equilibrium: The Logic of Choice and the Logic of Production', in I. M. Kirzner (ed.), *Subjectivism, Intelligibility and Economic Understanding. Essays in Honor of Ludwig M. Lachmann on his Eightieth Birthday* (London: Macmillan, 1986).

alternative quantities of money. It is accordingly a purely logical relation between interest rates and the stock of money. It has no implications for the controllability of money on the part of the central bank (i.e. for the exogenous or endogenous nature of money). It illustrates virtual states of equilibrium between money, which agents wish to hold in anticipation of a rise in the interest rate, and bonds, demanded in anticipation of its decline, given the state of the expectations. This last factor is the crucial determinant of the rate of interest, as it fixes the position of the curve which monetary policy must come to terms with.

The state of expectations depends on the available information ('state of the news') and on the prevailing model adopted by convention, that is, on the interest-forecasting structure which the market makes use of as the most convenient basis for action in a particular situation. The available information determines the conventional model and, by furnishing the values of the variables, its solution. Moreover, the available information determines the degree of confidence in the model. Liquidity preference changes, therefore, with the flow of information that generates new data to which the assumed conventional model is applied, and new evidence by which to judge the convenience of relying on it. These are the relevant changes which explain movements in the long-term rate of interest. They define what Keynes's theory seeks especially to highlight: the possibility on the part of economic policy to influence the conventional determination of the interest rate.

Unlike the neo-classical view, the analysis of this possibility is not based on reference to positions of natural equilibrium or disequilibrium. The markets are always in the conventional equilibrium described by the liquidity preference curve. Consequently, it is not based on reference to a condition of full employment.

Economic policy may have the power to direct the markets by shifting the relative weight of the different opinions of the agents, by dictating the conventional models markets cannot do without, and by governing the degree of confidence in them. Keynes places this potential control of the rate of interest in a fundamental asymmetry, lacking in neo-classical theory, that hinders downward but not upward movement. The downward rigidity of the long-term rate of interest is attributed in the first place not to inflation, but to the strength of the belief in conventions that appear as if rooted in 'objective grounds',[9] or to the uncertainty that keeps the liquidity preference high.

The attempt to cut the long-term rate of interest by increasing the money supply through open-market operations can be thwarted by the rigidity of expected rates, apparent in the interest elasticity of the speculative demand for money. This effort may also be frustrated by upward shifts in the demand for money generated by deteriorating expectations, by the failure to accept—which may stem from a failure to understand—the expansionary monetary action:

In dealing with the speculative-motive it is . . . important to distinguish between the changes in the rate of interest which are due to changes in the supply of money available to satisfy the speculative-motive, without there having been any change in the liquidity function, and those which are primarily due to changes in expectation affecting the liquidity function itself. Open-market operations may, indeed, influence the rate of interest through both channels; since they may not only change the volume of money, but may also give rise to changed expectations concerning the future policy of the Central Bank or of the Government.[10]

Even if the monetary policy is inadequate, the tools of economic policy in the hands of the state need not be so. It is the governments, together with central banks, who must provide the frame of reference for the market to develop its expectations and conventions. It is the governments who can, by generating projects for the future of society, reduce uncertainty and give strength and stability to favourable, positive conventions. The frame of reference that the state must provide to the financial markets is not limited to fiscal policy. It undoubtedly also includes the international monetary regime and its coordinated management, as well as the various possible configurations of

----

9 Keynes, op. cit., 204.   10 Ibid., 197–8.

he relations that in market economies link capital, labour, and inance (incomes policies, relations between industry and finance). Far from being exogenous historical and institutional ariables, in Keynes's mind these elements play a fundamental ole in determining the central banks' capacity to influence the ate of interest.

Nor is the structure of the financial system without importance. Keynes's reasoning rejects the Fisherian identity between inancial system and financial market. The system takes on orms that are historically determined, with significant differences across periods and countries. These differences influence he interest rate and its reactions to monetary policy, as asserted hroughout the *General Theory*.[11]

To broaden the terms of what is stated incidentally by Keynes, we take the *transactions approach* to money as a complement to, and not a substitute for, Keynes's fundamental *uncertainty approach*. Two distinctions are then relevant in dealing vith the structure of the financial market: the distinction etween customer and market relationships and that between fluid' investment (that of the professional or speculative investor in the Keynesian sense) and 'solid' investment (that of vidows and orphans).[12] The first distinction refers directly to he relative weight of bank credit and markets in a financial ystem; the second refers to the typology of investors and ntermediaries. The two distinctions converge in indicating that he theory of liquidity preference is the more significant the more inancial systems are oriented toward market relations with fluid' investors. As Hicks argues, the fluidity that characterizes nvestors managing their own portfolio with an eye to the profits obtainable from continuous trading can also depend on transaction costs that decrease with scale. Thus, the importance of

[11] Ibid., 159, 160, 172.

[12] J. R. Hicks, 'The Foundations of Monetary Theory', in *Collected Essays on Economic Theory*, vol. ii (*Money, Interest and Wages*) (Oxford: Basil Blackwell, 1982), h. 19. On the relation between the Keynesian and the Hicksian approaches to money, ee, however, J. A. Kregel, 'The Formation of Fix and Flex Prices and Monetary Theory: An Appraisal of John Hicks' *A Market Theory of Money*', *BNL Quarterly eview* (1990), 475–86.

liquidity preference increases with the financial saving entrusted
to institutional investors in capital markets.

The theory of liquidity preference also points to the volatility
of yields as a source of uncertainty which correspondingly
limits the downward flexibility of the interest rate. The tendency
to greater volatility is due in part to another important factor
noted by Keynes among the determinants of convention, and by
Hicks among the determinants of the fluidity of investment: the
international monetary system. The regime of flexible exchange
rates modifies the ways uncertainty manifests itself; it can also
increase uncertainty and with it the mutability of conventional
models. A monetary regime not based on pre-established rules
but on international cooperation that must continuously be
recreated, with developed and complex financial markets, is
intrinsically unstable.[13]

[13] J. R. Hicks, 'The Foundations', 275.

4

A Keynesian Reading
of World Interest Rates,
1970–1993

Keynes's theory of interest is even less amenable to direct econometric verification than its neo-classical counterpart. Instead of relying on a single predetermined model—as is the case with neo-classical propositions—Keynes's suggestion is to investigate the correspondence between time series evidence and not one but a variety of models reflecting the conventions markets have successively adopted, with changing degrees of confidence, in various circumstances. The profound difference in method, in content, and therefore in nature between the neo-classical theory and Keynes's approach is that the latter is not given to simple, direct empirical verification. It does not check the refutability of the hypotheses against the facts in the neo-positivist style.

Consistent with Keynes's method, we will attempt to identify the conventions which correspond to the major turning points in the time profile of interest rates by taking into consideration the main changes in the economic setting and the obstacles faced by economic policy. Such conventions can follow or overlap one another, exclude or generate one another, derive from factual evidence or stem from the sentiment of the market. We will examine the evolution of interest rates in this light and put forward explanations founded on the persuasiveness of the argument[1] rather than on econometric tests. The comparison

---

[1] Carabelli, op. cit., ch. 9, para. 2.

with the neo-classical position reviewed above will therefore be cast primarily in terms of the interpretative adequacy of an analysis that does not confine itself to a single model.

Given the monetary character of Keynes's theory, the immediate object of our analysis can only be the nominal rate of interest. Real rates will then be approached *ex post*, with a Keynesian appreciation of the will and capacity of central banks to maintain the long-term rate at a reasonably low and stable level, given the rate of inflation.

The *a priori*, general arguments supporting the notion and importance of conventions in determining interest rates are crucial. Those arguments can be corroborated by historical illustrations, identifying the specific conventions prevailing in the financial markets and their influence on the movement in interest rates observed in a period of time.

Our main purpose is the methodological one of reproposing Keynes's approach to interest rates, in an analytical environment presently dominated by simplified versions of the neo-classical paradigm. Rather than reconstructing the economic history of the 1970s and the 1980s, we intend to select the elements from that history which characterize the evolving framework within which the wide fluctuation in interest rates took place and monetary policy was enacted. Financial markets successively relied on the conventions shaped by these elements as they transformed the signals of monetary policies into the prices of long-term assets and thus into interest rates. The transition from one convention to another, like their occasional superimposition, is marked by the turning points with which history expresses the interaction of new facts with the reactions of economic policy. The reconstruction we present focuses on these turning points and sketches an outline of the evolution that connects them.

Most of the economic literature sees the events that we reconsider in terms of 'shocks', which supposedly affected economies that were otherwise functioning smoothly. But 'shock' is a highly ambiguous term. A disturbance or a positive change in the economy, despite apparent discontinuities, rarely lack roots in history, including distant history. The post-1968 wage 'explosion' resolved distributional disequilibria and political tensions that had been growing, especially in Europe, over the years. The declaration of the dollar's inconvertibility into gold in August 1971 and the crisis of the 'Bretton Woods' international monetary system had their precursors in the growth of the United States' foreign indebtedness with respect to its gold reserves;[2] to this was added from 1965, the incapacity to restrain domestic demand in the US economy against the inflationary stimulus of spending for the war in Vietnam. The energy crises of 1973 and 1979 had been preceded by twenty years of decline in real oil prices, dissipation of energy sources, and neglect of the economic and political problems faced by oil-producing countries.

Even with respect to the reunification of Germany in 1989, the term 'shock' proves to be simplistic and ill-suited to convey the last step of a long march towards reunification. The Federal Republic of Germany accomplished this process mainly by giving its foreign policy the support of a growing creditor position with respect to the rest of the world. The financial strength of Germany, projected overseas, was built up over decades in which a current balance of payments surplus was the prime objective of economic policy. This objective took on more importance than the external value of the mark and it became the ultimate purpose of price stability itself. The financial strength of Germany proved capable of obtaining the assent even of the political partners with the least enthusiasm for German reunification.[3]

In the Keynesian perspective, on the other hand, novel events and the changing problems they pose for economic policy constitute the new conventions that establish themselves in the financial markets. Four of these will be singled out in the

---

[2] R. Triffin, *Gold and the Dollar Crisis. The Future of Convertibility* (New Haven: Yale University Press, 1960).

[3] P. Ciocca and O. Vito Colonna, 'La politica economica della Germania federale e i suoi riflessi internazionali (1969–79)', in V. Valli (ed.), *L'economia tedesca* (Milan: Etas, 1981).

following paragraphs, to explain the fluctuations of the interest rate during the 1970s and the 1980s. These four conventions are linked to the following factors and events: the sudden end to the regular and sustained growth enjoyed by the world economy up to the early 1970s; the shift in the design and regime of monetary policy in the United States and elsewhere at the end of 1979; the double element of uncertainty that entered American economic policy from the early 1980s and the lack of consistency among the economic policies of the United States, Japan and Germany; and the fear, which from the late 1980s prevailed in the financial markets, that saving might not meet the demands of world investment.

We will illustrate each of the four conventions on the basis of the analytical choice made by Keynes in his treatment of monetary policy. In the *General Theory*, monetary policy is considered in the light of the sharp distinction between the short-term rate and the long-term rate. The central bank can act directly and effectively on the former; it can influence the latter only indirectly, through the market's expectations, including those concerning the sustainability of the stance of monetary management. This approach appears justified even when a 'monetarist convention' centred on the subjection of monetary expansion to quantitative limits and targets prevails. For the United States, for example, one can take the interest rate on the short-term Federal Funds market as the primary tool used by the central bank. This holds good even from October 1979 to October 1982, when the monetary policy regime changed radically. Despite the new quantitative control then employed by the Federal Reserve, only one-third of the variation of the Federal Funds rate was attributable to automatic factors of supply and demand. No less than two-thirds were, instead, traceable to discretionary interventions by the central bank.[4] In the German case, one can

---

[4] M. Goodfriend, 'Interest Rate Policy and the Inflation Scare Problem, 1979–1992', *FRB of Richmond Economic Quarterly* (1993), 1–24. This hypothesis is even more justified for the years 1983–7. With reference to this period, the quantitative objectives, first and foremost those referred to as M1, lost importance, in a context in which the monetary base, money in its various senses, and credit grew with respect to nominal

assume that despite the Bundesbank's apparent acceptance of monetarist precepts since December 1974,[5] the maintenance of interest rates at high and stable levels continued to represent the course of monetary regulation of the economy. More generally, to be sure, for any economy 'at a deeper level there is an equivalence between talking in terms of interest rates or money'.[6]

THE INFLATION OF THE 1970S

Early in the 1970s the world economy abandoned the apparently tranquil conditions then prevailing. The industrial countries had grown with exceptional regularity at an average rate of 5 per cent per annum, with inflation under 4 per cent, real long-term interest rates not above 2 per cent, relatively inactive monetary policies, and a normally flat term structure of interest rates. The most evident and most discussed manifestation of the crisis, along with the imbalances of the international payments system, was the combination of stagnation and inflation. Despite the analytical ambiguity of the notion of 'shock', it struck markets as something new, something which marked a break with respect to the trends of the world economy in the 1950s and 1960s. The stable pattern of the first twenty post-war years was replaced by another pattern corresponding to the low, and even negative, real interest rates that prevailed from the early 1970s almost to the end of the decade.

Sudden increases in the average price level such as those

income and prices much more than the previous trends would have suggested (see B. Friedman, 'Lessons on Monetary Policy from the 1980s', *Journal of Economic Perspectives* (1988), 51–72). The decision to view the formulation of US monetary policy in those years in terms of interest rates rather than money supply is also suggested by the difficulty, admittedly not an insuperable one, of 'repairing the money demand function' in that economy. For an attempt in this direction see W. Poole, 'Monetary Policy Lessons of Recent Inflation and Disinflation', *Journal of Economic Perspectives* (1988), 73–100.

[5] The Bundesbank has always defined its monetarism as 'pragmatic', in the style of central bankers rather than of 'Chicago school' theorists. See Emminger, op. cit., 145.

[6] Goodfriend, op. cit., 5.

which occurred in 1974 and 1979 can provoke an immediate erosion of the real interest rate, as foreseen by Fisher. But the decline in real rates was not the mechanical result of a surge in inflation with no change in the 'natural' equilibrium. Rather, it stemmed from an economic policy far more concerned with losses of output and employment than with inflation.

The economic problem involved in choosing between alternative objectives, or the lesser of two evils, is fully consistent with the analysis that prevailed at the time. In the mainstream macroeconomics of the neo-classical synthesis,[7] indeed, wage claims, the increases in oil prices, and even the instability of exchange rates were seen as 'shocks' that reduced the aggregate supply of goods and services in the industrial economies so that an anti-inflationary reduction in aggregate demand would seriously magnify the fall in production and employment.[8]

Policy makers and markets shared the conviction that the policy choice had to be, or in any case would be, to defend employment against supply shocks. This is the First Convention that can be identified following the breakdown in the equilibria that had characterized the first two post-war decades.

Fiscal policies were accommodating. Large, or larger, public deficits were accepted, especially during the first oil crisis. In 1975 the G-7 budget deficits reached 4.4 per cent of GDP, from balances that were barely negative in 1972–4. A tendency to reduce the deficits appeared only after 1983 and it would come to a halt in 1990.

Monetary policies had been quite restrictive in 1972–3, especially in Germany and France. Short-term rates rose, absolutely and with respect to long-term rates, to reach 14 and 11 per

---

[7] On the interpretations of the crisis of the 1970s see P. Ciocca, *L'instabilità dell'economia* (Turin: Einaudi, 1987), ch. 3.

[8] 'In the case of supply shocks, there is no miracle cure, there is no macro policy which can both maintain a stable price level and keep employment at its natural rate. To maintain stable prices in the face of the exogenous price shock, say a rise in import prices, would require a fall in all domestic output prices; but we know of no macro policy by which domestic prices can be made to fall except by creating enough slack, thus putting downward pressure on wages.' F. Modigliani, 'The Monetarist Controversy or, Should We Forsake Stabilization Policies?', *American Economic Review* (1977), 15.

cent in nominal terms, and 7 and 3 per cent in real terms, respectively. The subsequent policy stance was not to be rigid in the face of the jumps in oil prices; it aimed at gradually reabsorbing their inflationary repercussions. In the months following the two so-called oil shocks, as inflation began to slow down after the impact of the higher primary product prices, real interest rates did not reach 2 per cent. This occurred even though they rose from negative levels and short-term rates increased faster than long-term rates. In the G-7 aggregate, the money supply (in its widest acceptation) grew at sustained annual rates, near 14 per cent in 1972–4, and 12 in 1975–9.

The management and understanding of the international monetary system were marked by the fear of traumatic interruptions in the recycling of 'petrodollars'. The recycling was carried out, in fact, more through market mechanisms than through official financial transactions. Between 1973 and 1977 bank crises were quite frequent; they included the 'fringe banks' in Britain, the Herstatt in Germany, the Franklin and the Security National Bank of Long Island in the United States, and the state-owned, medium-term credit institutions in Italy. The crises raised fears regarding the solidity of the financial structure and the willingness to protect it with liquidity creation.

The conviction that the fixed-exchange-rate regime could not last and that it was imperative to find new degrees of freedom in the relations among currencies gradually made headway, albeit through a difficult process of trial and error, and finally became dominant. Exchange rate flexibility received legal sanction with the modifications of Article 4 of the code of the International Monetary Fund in Kingston, Jamaica, in February 1976. The United States accepted a halving of the value of the dollar with respect to the German mark and the yen between the start of the decade and 1978–9. Europe gave up the 'Werner Plan' for monetary unification in 1972–3; a new commitment to cohesion among the major European currencies would reappear only in 1978–9, with the European Monetary System (EMS). The anti-inflationary discipline inherent in fixed exchange rates was abandoned.

In the United States inflation remained high, between 6 and 11 per cent annually, in 1974–9. In the leading economy it was gradually realized that one now lived 'in a world in which the success of American policies would be dependent on the complementary policies of others'.[9] But for the extreme reached in 1977–9, with the Carter Administration's 'locomotive theory', American economic diplomacy moved consistently to achieve external commercial and financial equilibrium through demand growth in Germany and Japan rather than through policies of severity at home.

In an essay significantly entitled *The Anguish of Central Banking*, Arthur Burns, chairman of the board of governors of the Federal Reserve System from 1970 to 1978, summed up the feelings of those responsible for economic and monetary policy in the United States and elsewhere. His tone was sincere, truthful, and thus disarming and almost apologetic. In those years inflation appeared inevitable and so the lesser evil. It seemed ultimately rooted in the 'philosophic and political currents of thought that have impinged on economic life since the Great Depression and particularly since the mid-1960s'.[10] The markets eventually reflected this climate: higher nominal interest rates, given inflation and expected inflation, were to be considered improbable not least because of the widespread fear of their possible repercussions on economic activity, employment, and the systemic stability of banking and financial intermediation. Economic policies and market expectations combined to depress real interest rates as had never happened in two centuries, excepting the sharp inflations during and after the two World Wars.

The term structure of interest rates gradually shifted. Long rates became normally higher than short-term rates. The exceptions were the episodes of relatively scarce liquidity in the

[9] P. A. Volcker and T. Gyohten, *Changing Fortunes. The World's Money and the Threat to American Leadership* (New York: Random House, 1992), 146. Ample reference will be made to this book, in view of the direct testimony it offers from two leading actors, respectively American and Japanese.

[10] A. F. Burns, 'The Anguish of Central Banking', in P. Ciocca (ed.), *Money and the Economy*, 162.

immediate aftermath of the two oil crises. In the context of reduced output growth, the change in the term structure reflected
the rise in expected inflation to levels well above those of the
1950s and 1960s. Long-term interest rates nonetheless failed to
anticipate inflation fully. The decade ended with real interest
rates that declined to negative values in 1979–80, as they did
earlier in 1974–5: minus 2 per cent in the G-7, with lows near
minus 4 per cent in the United States and Italy. Far from being
considered a temporary phenomenon, inflation was accepted by
both policy-makers and markets.

'TAKING ON INFLATION', 1979–1983

The quotation in this section title is, appropriately, from Paul A.
Volcker, who headed US central banking from August 1979 to
September 1987.[11] With Volcker's appointment the monetary
policy of the United States underwent an immediate and radical
change. It became harshly restrictive in its procedures and,
above all, it was pursued intensely. The fight against inflation
took priority.

The turning point can be dated to the secret meeting of the
Open Market Committee of the Federal Reserve on Saturday, 6
October 1979. It was signalled by the increase of the discount
rate to 13 per cent in February 1980 and to 14 per cent in May
1981. It manifested itself with a twin surge in short-term
nominal interest rates and in the entire yield curve early in 1980
and again in the summer of 1981: 'One telltale sign of our
difficulties was that when short-term rates rose, as anticipated,
long-term rates did, too. If the markets were convinced that
inflation would be coming down, presumably that would not
have happened, at least not for long'.[12]

An analogous and nearly contemporaneous redirection of
monetary policy took place in other countries. In Italy the

[11] Volcker and Gyohten, op. cit., 163.   [12] Ibid., 170.

economic and political situation was even more difficult than in the United States, and the independent move of the central bank was effected by different technical means. Between October 1979 and March 1981 the new governor of the Bank of Italy, Carlo A. Ciampi, raised the discount rate from 10.5 to 19 per cent, the highest level in Italy's monetary history. In November 1981 long-term interest rates exceeded 21 per cent.

Over and above the events specific to single central banks and single countries, after the second oil crisis the fight against inflation was conducted with greater determination. Everywhere, there was a growing fear that the inflation which had become entrenched in the 1970s might accelerate out of control. In a number of countries, the trade-off with unemployment came to be seen as less onerous. The strictly neo-classical monetarist critique of the neo-classical synthesis spread beyond academic circles to governments and parliaments. Financial markets adopted a new convention—the Second Convention—that focused on inflation and on the monetary expansion which, according to monetarist doctrine, was its main determinant. For the markets, the shift in the Federal Reserve's policy stance meant uncertainty as to the (higher) level of interest rates needed to curb inflation in the new monetary policy regime.[13]

In part because of the accumulation of public debt over the decade, even fiscal policies were less accommodating in 1979–80 than in 1974–5. Above all, monetary policy was far more severely restricted, and not just in the United States and Italy. In the G-7, average inflation in consumer prices peaked at 12.7 per cent in 1980, not far below the rate of 13.8 per cent reached in 1974; average short-term nominal interest rates approached 14 per cent in 1981, whereas in 1974–5 they had barely exceeded 8 per cent. Although the increase in long-term nominal rates was much sharper than the increase which took

13 P. Davidson, 'A Post-Keynesian View of Theories and Causes for High Real Interest Rates', in P. Arestis (ed.), *Post-Keynesian Monetary Economics. New Approaches to Financial Modelling* (Aldershot: Elgar, 1988), describes Volcker's change of direction in terms of 'an uncertain (non-ergodic) environment where past time series evidence provided little statistical reliability in forecasting the quantitative changes in future nominal interest rates' (175).

place after the first oil crisis, the differential between short-term and long-term rates was not dissimilar—about half of one per cent. At both current and constant prices, the overall growth in the money stock in the leading countries was much smaller and it was slowing down.

Real interest rates rose from the negative levels of 1979. Owing, among other things, to the mechanical effect of the drop in inflation following the initial impact of the increases in the price of oil, they continued to rise beyond the 1981 peak of the nominal rates, reaching a maximum of about 7 per cent in 1983. After oscillating around this figure in 1983–4, they began to fall slowly.

These events provide confirmation of the fundamental asymmetry noted by Keynes in the *General Theory*: that whereas monetary policy cannot always reduce 'recalcitrant'[14] long-term interest rates because it is hindered by uncertain, pessimistic, or inflationary expectations, it can under almost any condition cause an increase in the price of money.

In the G-7, inflation fell from 12.6 per cent in 1980 to 4.7 per cent in 1983. This fall accompanied a mediocre growth in production, under 2 per cent annually in 1980–1, which turned into the recession of 1982. Apart from 1975, this was the only year since the war which saw an absolute decline (–0.3 per cent) in the gross domestic product of the G-7. The very high and rising interest rates played an important part in determining the outcome.

THE TWIN CONTRADICTIONS IN THE GOVERNMENT OF THE WORLD ECONOMY

Under the 'monetarist convention' established by the shift in monetary policy, the markets had become particularly sensitive

---

[14] 'The long-term rate may be more recalcitrant when once it has fallen to a level which, on the basis of past experience and present expectations of *future* monetary policy, is considered "unsafe" by representative opinion. For example, in a country

to any sign of renewed inflation, as well as becoming uncertain about the future path of interest rates. But this seems inadequate to explain the further rise in real rates in 1982–3, and, above all, the slow pace of their decline over the ensuing four years. The sharp and almost continuous decline in inflation weakened the 'monetarist convention' and reduced uncertainty. Nonetheless, the fall in long-term nominal rates was gradual. Even in 1986, the year with the lowest recorded inflation in the entire 1960–93 period, the G-7 real interest rate was still about twice its average level of the 1960s.

The evolution of interest rates over the 1980s makes sense in terms of a Third Convention, which introduced a double uncertainty, as yet not overcome. This stemmed from the appearance, and then the persistence, of twin contradictions in the government of the world economy. The contradictions were internal and external to the United States, which, though still the world's largest economy, found itself increasingly sensitive to the economic policies of countries like Germany and Japan.

Within the United States, the conflict was between an expansionary fiscal policy and an anti-inflationary monetary policy. Notwithstanding the first Reagan Administration's supply-side notions that tax cuts would boost revenues, fiscal policy actually led to some of the largest deficits in American history. Monetary policy was engaged in eradicating inflation, with 'ferociously high interest rates' in 1981 and only *ex post* doubts 'about whether we weren't too slow to ease in 1982'.[15] In the Federal Reserve's interpretation, the budget deficits reduced domestic saving in an economy already suffering from slow investment and productivity growth, large commercial and current account external deficits, and a deterioration of the country's net financial position. The latter was so rapid that it transformed the

linked to an international gold standard, a rate of interest lower than prevails elsewhere will be viewed with a justifiable lack of confidence; yet a domestic rate of interest dragged up to a parity with the *highest* rate (highest after allowing for risk) prevailing in any country belonging to the international system may be much higher than is consistent with domestic full employment.' Keynes, op. cit., 203.

[15] Volcker and Gyohten, op. cit., 176–7.

United States from the world's major net creditor into its major net debtor. The calls for reduction in the budget deficits became a *leitmotiv* of the central bank's statements, classified as well as public. The Administration's position was instead optimistic: 'The more starry-eyed Reaganauts argued that reducing taxes would provide a kind of magic elixir for the economy that would make the deficits go away, or at least not matter'.[16]

The fundamental contradiction inherent in the combination of an expansionary fiscal policy and a restrictive monetary policy manifested itself in an extraordinary appreciation of the dollar as interest rates in the United States rose above those in the other countries. Between 1979 and February 1985, the average effective value of the dollar increased by some 40 per cent, with an enormous loss of price competitiveness for the United States.

Economists and even commentators were divided into two schools. Some believed that a reduction in the budget deficit would have induced a decline in interest rates and a re-equilibrating depreciation of the dollar. Others, on the contrary, believed that it would have further strengthened the dollar by increasing confidence in the future of the American economy. Unhappily, there was no chance to test the hypothesis. The budget deficit remained high; furthermore, between 1980 and 1993, the public debt rose from 38 to 65 per cent of the gross domestic product.

Outside the United States, the contradiction was no less acute. The appreciation of the dollar made it easy for the exports from competing economies, notably Japan and Germany, to penetrate the American market. The trading partners' surplus on current account accompanied major foreign purchases of income-yielding assets in the United States through direct and portfolio investments by non-residents, mainly Japanese.

Following the post-war tradition of the Republican Party then in power, American economic diplomacy eschewed protectionist measures. However, it did put pressure on the partners to limit their exports and stimulate their imports, both directly and

[16] Ibid., 177.

through more expansionary fiscal and monetary policies. In structurally export-led economies like that of Germany and, above all, Japan, this action should have gone hand in hand with a redirection of growth towards domestic demand. The main partners of the United States put up a stubborn resistance, even in periods like 1980–3, when the European economy appeared to be suffering from 'sclerosis', with growth rates oscillating around 1 per cent per year, and the Japanese economy growing at 3 per cent, well below its potential. The advantages of commercial and financial penetration into the United States—not merely economic—were accompanied by the conviction that less wary monetary and fiscal policies in Europe and Japan would jeopardise the stability of domestic and international prices.

The inconsistency between the trends and economic policies of the United States on the one hand and Japan and Germany on the other persisted in what the markets perceived as an unresolved conflict, overt or latent. The precarious nature of the apparent equilibrium is confirmed by at least two problems that came to the fore, again within and outside the United States. The very independence of the US central bank, under pressure from the Administration to pursue a less rigorous policy, appeared exposed more than once to 'ominous threats' and 'mysterious studies' of institutional reform.[17] The combination of a strong dollar and high nominal and real interest rates made the foreign debt of the Third World countries a potentially destabilizing factor for the international banking system. This became obvious in August 1982, when Mexico's 'illiquidity' endangered a number of large banks beyond the Continental Illinois, which was already threatened by the affair of the Penn Square National Bank of Oklahoma. Categories apparently forgotten since the days of Bagehot, like 'illiquidity-insolvency' and 'lender of last resort', had to be rapidly rediscovered and translated into effective supporting measures, with implications in terms of discretionary choices, the mingling of technical and political elements, and uncertainty.

[17] Ibid., 175.

Though less ambiguous a term than 'shock', 'uncertainty', too, is not unequivocal. Yet, in the light of the reading of events which we have proposed, it acquires a clear-cut meaning if it is placed in the context of Keynes's theory of interest:

A monetary policy which strikes public opinion as being experimental in character or easily liable to change may fail in its objective of greatly reducing the long-term rate of interest, because M_2 may tend to increase almost without limit in response to a reduction of "r" below a certain figure.[18]

From the early 1980s, monetary policies appeared increasingly overburdened with tasks, constraints, and preoccupations. They were therefore manifestly *unsafe*, in Keynes's sense, to the extent that they passed beyond the stage of clear and unmistakable restriction. Their basic stance remained cautious even when they allowed a decline in short-term nominal interest rates, in keeping with the concomitant decline in inflation. There was a failure to make them part of a policy mix that would be consistent within each economy and also, perhaps more importantly, in terms of the relations between the various countries' economic policies. They proved incapable of providing a framework for an effective, credible government of the world economy.

These opposing influences, potentially capable of reorienting monetary policies in one direction or another, introduced an element of pure uncertainty. The effect was to increase the demand for money. Other things being equal, this could be offset only by a premium, which increases the upward slope of the yield curve. When monetary policies became less restrictive in an effort to sustain the economy or banking and financial intermediaries, the markets feared that the new stance could not be maintained. The result was downward rigidity of real long-term interest rates.

After the worst of the monetary restriction in 1982, the prevalence of an upward-sloping term structure confirms the

---

[18] Keynes, op. cit., 203.

existence of an illiquidity premium. As we shall see in the next section, long-term nominal rates often rose, or failed to fall, when central banks drove short-term rates down: the expectations that monetary policies were reversible prevailed.

THE RESTRAINED DECLINE IN INTEREST RATES, 1984–1987

In a sense, real interest rates could only recede from the peak levels they reached in 1983. Their fall stemmed from a decline in nominal rates that exceeded the decline in current and expected inflation. Various factors were involved. The highly restrictive stance of the monetary policy in the early 1980s was somewhat attenuated, even though caution continued to prevail. The fall in inflation justified the loosening of policy while it reduced one of the main sources of uncertainty and expectations of future monetary and credit restrictions. The relative or 'real' prices of primary products tended downwards. Crude oil prices diminished so sharply in 1986 that there was talk of an oil 'counter-shock', provoking the fall of that year's G-7 inflation rate to 2.1 per cent. The developing countries' debt crisis was managed in such a way as gradually to reduce the likelihood of an immediate and generalized crisis of the debtor countries and therefore of the creditor banks, despite difficulties and hesitations among repayment, rescheduling, and remission of the debt.

The decline in interest rates was restrained by the persistence, at the root of market expectations, of the convention dominated by the twin contradictions that had emerged between fiscal policy and monetary and exchange policy in the United States, and between the economic policies of the United States on the one hand and those of Japan and Germany on the other.

The United States persisted in running large deficits. Between 1984 and 1987 budget deficits remained near 3 per cent of gross product and there was a deterioration in the ratio of saving to investment in the private sector. Interest rates remained high and the dollar continued to appreciate until 1985, contributing to the further increase in the external deficit on current account. The central bank never ceased to worry about the 'twin deficits': the budget deficit and the balance of payments deficit. After 1985 it also feared the inflationary effect of an excessive or overrapid depreciation of the dollar. Monetary policy therefore remained prudent. Even when the degree of restriction was eased, the markets considered the more expansionary stance 'unsafe' and reversible due to the risk of inflation and the central bank's determination to act to contain such risks. At the same time the domestic and international economic policy of the second Reagan Administration tended to bring the dollar down from its high level, thus pressing objectively for a reduction in interest rates or at least for a postponement of further credit restrictions.

The Treasury and the Central Bank agreed that America's loss of competitiveness and the penetration of foreign goods and capital meant that a depreciation of the dollar could not be avoided. Among other things, there would otherwise have been a strengthening of the protectionist pressures, always latent in American society and already widely voiced in Congress, dominated by a Democratic majority. But the Bank considered a reduction in the budget deficit a preliminary condition for a non-inflationary devaluation of the exchange rate, while the Treasury was set on accepting the devaluation in any case. The Federal Reserve's insistence that the deficit be reduced continued to fall on deaf ears. Though nominal and real interest rates declined, both absolutely and with respect to Japanese and German levels, the Federal Reserve's dissatisfaction with the lax fiscal policy and its concern for the possible inflationary effect of the dollar depreciation were perfectly clear to the markets. This meant that a monetary restriction and a rise in interest rates could occur at any time.

In its relations with Japan and Germany, the United States

pursued three intermediate objectives: to encourage, and gain acceptance for, the depreciation of the dollar ('Plaza' agreement, New York, September 1985); to induce other countries to expand domestic demand (Tokyo summit, May 1986; 'Louvre' agreement, Paris, February 1987, which was also aimed at fixing the dollar at the lowest levels it had reached); and to put pressure on Japan to adopt the radical reforms needed to open its internal marketing and distribution systems to imported goods. With respect to interest rate differentials and the dollar, the intermediate objectives were fully achieved: in 1985–6 short-term rates declined from 8.5 to 5.5 per cent in the United States and from 6 to 4.5 per cent in Japan and Germany, while the dollar lost a third of its value before levelling out in 1987–8. With respect to budgetary policies they were achieved only in part: Germany's policy set off only a slight and temporary expansionary impulse (under 1 per cent of GDP), while Japan's policy remained restrictive. With respect to the structural, microeconomic reforms of the Japanese market, so inviting and so closed, they were not achieved at all. One could not expect rapid, significant results from the 'Maekawa Plan' of 1986 itself,[19] drafted by the highly respected former governor of the Bank of Japan, Haruo 'Mike' Maekawa. The plan put forth important proposals to open the Japanese market to imports and to reorient the entire development model of the Japanese economy, traditionally centred on exports, towards domestic demand. It met strenuous resistance from specific vested interests rooted in Japanese society.

The ultimate objective—the restoration of equilibrium in the balance of payments on current account—was entirely missed. The leading country of the world economy, far from returning to surplus and thus exporting real resources to the rest of the world, continued to incur current account deficits of about 3 per cent of GDP and to cumulate external debt. If the third intermediate objective was unreachable in the short term, the first and second struck America's partners as frankly contradictory,

[19] *The Report of the Advisory Group on Economic Structural Adjustment for International Harmony* (Tokyo, 5 April 1986).

given that the United States itself lacked the will to reduce its budget deficit.[20]

The twin contradictions of the policy mix, within the United States and abroad, limited the will and the ability of the monetary authorities to promote lower real long-term interest rates as well the willingness of the financial markets to apply these rates. On at least two occasions—in 1983–4 and in 1986–7—one in the United States, the other at an international level, the reductions in short-term rates not only failed to affect long-term rates, but actually led to upward tendencies in the long rates.

In the spring of 1980 the United States had already witnessed a temporary change toward expansion in the restrictive stance of monetary policy. In March of that year banks' consumer credit had been subject to severe administrative controls. Consumption immediately fell, reducing GDP by 10 per cent, at an annual rate, in the second quarter. As an automatic result of the decreased demand for money, and thanks also to the discretionary expansion enacted by the Federal Reserve, short-term rates fell suddenly from 17.6 per cent in March to 9 per cent in July, when even the credit controls were removed; long-term rates declined only 2.5 points and went back up when short-term rates fell below them and the gap touched around one percentage point (Fig. 4). Inflation in those months remained at double-digit levels (13 per cent annually). The market feared inflation and expected the Federal Reserve to return to its anti-inflationary stance as soon as the temporary fall in production had been overcome. In 1980, the government budget began to undergo a long period of uninterrupted deficits.

After 1980, the first significant episode in the United States

---

[20] In the words of a leading Japanese figure, Toyoo Gyohten: 'From the Japanese and German viewpoints, the whole process was frustrating because we thought that the United States was trying to gain political concessions from the surplus countries of Japan and Germany by using the threat of talking down the dollar and the threat of protectionism, knowing that both could really damage the economies of the surplus countries . . . Our response therefore was defensive and displayed a lack of willingness to contribute positively to the global economic benefit. In other words, regrettably, there was a serious lack of mutual trust among the three major countries.' Volcker and Gyohten, op. cit., 263.

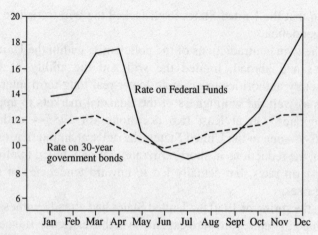

Fig. 4. Interest rates in the United States, 1980

Source: M. Goodfriend, 'Interest rate policy and the inflation scare problem, 1979–1992', unpublished typescript.

occurred in 1983–4. In mid-1982 the Federal Reserve had already eased the monetary squeeze. It was faced with a fall in output of 2.2 per cent a year that it had itself induced by its anti-inflation policy and with a continuous decline in inflation, which would fall to less than 4 per cent in 1983. The decline in the nominal rates continued to the end of the year, when a cyclical recovery was initiated, becoming very rapid as early as the second quarter of 1983. Over the entire first half of 1983 the Federal Reserve kept short-term interest rates below 9 per cent, and then drove them up, anticyclically, to a peak of 11.6 per cent in August of 1984; the market, nonetheless, discounted an 'excessive' anti-inflationary reaction on the part of the Federal Reserve, almost as if it were offsetting the procyclical error made in the first semester of 1983 and with an eye to the magnitude (3–4 per cent of GDP) reached by the budget deficit. Long-term rates grew from 10.5 per cent in the first months of 1983 to 13.4 of June 1984, faster than short-term rates (Fig. 5). The budget deficit increased, even though it might occasionally shrink when the economy was cyclically strong.

The second episode dates from 1986–7 and is closely tied to

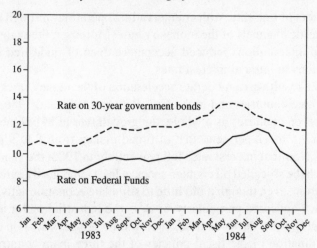

Fig. 5. Interest rates in the United States, 1983–1984

Source: M. Goodfriend, 'Interest rate policy and the inflation scare problem, 1979–1992', unpublished typescript.

the lack of coordination among the economic policies of the three major countries. Between the 'Plaza' and 'Louvre' agreements the United States failed to reduce its budget deficit. It put maximum pressure on Germany and Japan to accept the depreciation of the dollar and to pursue policies, monetary as well as fiscal, aimed at expanding domestic demand. A monetary policy that sharply reduced mark and yen interest rates would appear a hindrance to the depreciation of the dollar. Beyond certain limits, however, the latter did not please Japanese and German exporters.[21] To limit the appreciation of their currencies, the central banks of Germany and Japan intervened to buy dollars to the tune of 8 per cent of the stock of monetary base in 1986, and of 26 and 17 per cent, respectively, in 1987. These interventions became so large as to be hard to offset as

[21] 'Baker used foreign concern over dollar depreciation to advocate interest-rates cuts abroad, which would reduce dollar depreciation. He then used foreign interest-rate cuts to urge the Federal Reserve to follow a more expansionary policy in the United States.' W. Poole, 'Exchange-rate Management and Monetary Policy Mismanagement: A Study of Germany, Japan, and United States after Plaza', Carnegie–Rochester Conference Series on Public Policy (1992), no. 36, 64.

creators of liquidity, with countervailing operations through the domestic channels of the monetary base. Moreover, the scale of these interventions induced acceptance even of undesired reductions in internal interest rates.

The result was a moderate acceleration of the money stock in the three countries and in the G-7. Between 1985 and 1986, in the seven countries as a whole, the growth rate of M1 climbed from 9.5 to 12 per cent, that of broad money from 8 to 9 per cent. Nominal interest rates fell perceptibly in 1986, the year in which the so-called oil counter-shock at least temporarily curbed inflation, even though it did little to stimulate economic activity (which appeared particularly weak in the industrial sector and in Europe). At the same time, there was no progress at all in the coordination of the fiscal policies of the three main countries and, as seen above, there would be very little progress in 1987.

In the markets' evaluation, it was even clearer that the convergence of monetary policies was imposed by the United States and accepted unwillingly by Japan, and especially by Germany, and that fiscal policies remained inconsistent. Even though short-term rates were relatively low and falling, in the spring of 1987 long-term rates started climbing again in the United States, in Japan and in Germany. Once under way, the increase in rates proved rapid, especially *vis-à-vis* the declining trend in equity yields in the principal stock markets. Nevertheless, the rise in long-term interest rates was confirmed in August and September. In the United States the upward movement was then also fuelled by a fear of renewed inflation: the Federal Reserve raised the discount rate from 5.5 to 6 per cent early in September. Similar fears, resulting from the overshooting of monetary targets because of the intervention to support the dollar in the first half of the year, induced the Japanese authorities to limit the growth of bank loans and the Bundesbank to press for an increase in short-term market rates. Early in October monetary conditions became even harsher in Germany, following the half point increase in the reference rate for repurchase open market operations, and in the United States in an effort to support the exchange.

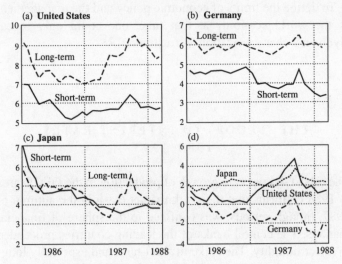

Fig. 6. Long- and short-term interest rates (A, B, C) and differential between returns on bonds and shares (D) in the United States, Germany, and Japan, 1986–1988 (monthly averages)

Source: Banca d'Italia, *Annual Reports*, various years.

The events of 1986–7 cannot be dismissed as a mere case of 'monetary policy mismanagement', as a 'classic cycle in interest rates, economic activity and inflation' in Friedman's monetarist style, attributable to a simultaneous and deliberate, if not coordinated, expansionary monetary policy.[22] In those two years the contradictions inherent in the economic policy of the United States and its partners culminated in increases in long-term interest rates, absolutely, relative to short-term rates, and relative to stock yields (Fig. 6).

On 19/20 October 1987, stock indices fell 21 per cent in New York and Tokyo and 17 per cent in London. Even if overbought to various degrees, stock markets shared an inability to bear the upward pressure on long-term rates resulting from the double 'tug of war' between fiscal and monetary policy in the United States and between the economic policies of the world's three major economies.

22 Ibid., 57.

To define the limits of economic policy and the management of the world economy at that time, one could only repeat Gyohten's characterization—'frustrating'.[23]

THE 'FLOOR' TO INTEREST RATES, 1988–1993

The robust 4.4 per cent growth of production in the OECD area in 1988 confirms that the stock market crash in the autumn of 1987, though serious, was confined to the sphere of financial markets. The central banks of the leading countries proceeded to inject liquidity. The spike in short-term and especially long-term nominal rates, which in October had burst the stock market bubble, was rapidly reabsorbed. Nonetheless, by the spring of 1988 short-term nominal interest rates were again climbing and long-term rates followed suit a little later. The halting downward path followed by real interest rates in 1984–7 came to an end. Short-term and long-term real interest rates settled at the relatively high average of 4 per cent or so, with modest variations (higher values in 1990 and 1992, lower ones in 1988–9, in 1991 and 1993).

In the Keynesian reading we are attempting, this unusual downward rigidity of real interest rates—representing a hard

[23] 'The period following the Louvre was frustrating as instability increased in the market. To the news media it seemed evident that policy coordination was not working. The rift deepened between the United States and Germany on monetary policy, with Secretary Baker repeatedly goading the German authorities to loosen, which they declined to do. Finally the markets revolted, and stock prices collapsed on Wall Street and throughout the world on October 19, Black Monday. The crash drew forth a multitude of explanations, but I am convinced that one fundamental cause was the failure to achieve real results in coordinating the macroeconomic policies of the seven major economic powers. In August of that year, the United States had amended the Graam-Rudmann-Hollings Act [of 1985] to postpone the target year for balancing the federal budget from 1991 to 1993. The budget deficit was actually declining, but it was improving far more slowly than the market hoped. The external accounts of the United States, Japan, and Germany did not improve at all, and the American external deficit even increased in 1987.' Volcker and Gyohten, op. cit., 268–9.

floor—can be attributed to a combination of forces. Cyclical and, so to speak, fortuitous factors interacted with the enduring fundamental disequilibrium represented by the budget and current account deficits of the United States. To these was added, with an independent significance in the markets' valuation, not the inadequacy, but the *expectation* of an inadequacy, in world savings with respect to the needs of investment, presumed to be rapidly growing in the medium term. A new convention, in Keynes's sense, therefore took shape. A Fourth Convention was added to the Third, and not as replacement to it: expectations of an essentially neo-classical character, paradoxically held at a time when the industrial economies were sliding toward a recession, with under-utilized productive capacity and an excess of current saving over current investment. As we have seen, Keynes's *general* theory of interest did not exclude a 'neo-classical convention', but rather explicitly allowed for it.

The long expansion that began in 1983 culminated in a growth of product that exceeded forecasts in 1988 and fell just short in 1989 (3.3 per cent). Inflation in consumer prices accelerated from 3 per cent in the first half of 1988 to 4.2 per cent in March 1989 and 5.5 per cent that May. Fiscal policies failed to exert a moderating influence on demand. Incomes policies seemed unlikely to limit the reaction of wages to the increases in non-oil primary product prices. In such a context, and perhaps overestimating the risk of inflation, monetary policies turned again toward restriction. They helped push into recession the British and American economies, where the heavily indebted private sector was particularly vulnerable to a fall in the yield of assets and a high cost of money. The restrictive monetary stance was maintained until the spring of 1989, past the cyclical turning point into recession, in the United States; it persisted in Japan to combat the asset price inflation and in Germany to contain the demand and wage inflation sparked by monetary unification (1 July 1990); and it came to be linked to the need to counteract the sharp increases in oil prices stemming from the crisis, and then the war, in the Persian Gulf (August 1990–February 1991).

The 'twin deficits' of the United States were not corrected. The budget deficit, which had dropped to 1.5 per cent of GDP in 1989, rose again, boosted by the recession, to a peak of 4.7 per cent in 1992. The external deficit on current account was only temporarily reduced by that same recession and, in 1991, by the official transfers paid over to the United States as financial contribution to their direct and preponderant commitment in the war against Iraq. The reabsorption of the bilateral trade deficit with Japan was certainly not favoured by the rise of the dollar against the yen by 30 per cent between late 1988 and the spring of 1990. Later that year, the dollar weakened again only because the expected cyclical upturn of the American economy failed to materialize and because dollar interest rates fell below the rising short-term interest rates in the other major currencies. In 1992 the US federal debt reached 51 per cent of product, against 27 per cent at the start of the 1980s. In the official projections assuming unchanged legislation, it was estimated that the debt could reach 58 per cent in 1998 and 66 per cent in 2002. The country's net debt to the rest of the world grew year by year, reaching at the end of 1992 a total, excluding gold reserves, of 550 billion dollars. All long-term projections discounted persistent deficits on current account in the balance of payments of the American economy.[24]

But the major new element that consolidated the expectations that the real cost of money would remain relatively high was the spreading concern with a world-wide shortage of saving.

At the start, this fear found a superficial justification in the very peak of the long cyclical expansion. Between 1983 and 1989 gross fixed investment in the OECD area had again increased in proportion to output. The strictly cyclical nature of the intense accumulation in 1988–9 is nonetheless manifest: despite the rapid growth of the capital stock, the rate of capacity utilization in the major countries then reached, and in some cases surpassed, the levels achieved in 1979–80, at the peak of the previous cyclical expansion. From a structural perspective,

---

[24] See, for example, the WEFA Group, *World Economic Outlook*, April 1993, 2–3.

in both industrialized and backward countries, a clear tendency had developed over time toward lower *ex post* gross and especially net saving. In the major economies the relatively substantial growth rates of output accompanied a sharp drop in public saving and a decline even in household saving, not offset by higher company profits.[25]

The downward tendency of the propensity to save suggested a risk of inadequate saving next to the investment needs that many considered urgent, high and growing, in mature economies as in the Third World.

Even in the United States there was a growing debate about the need to renew a capital stock that had probably become obsolete and certainly distorted and inefficient, notably in the public sector. Though some thought it sufficient to eliminate the distortions and inefficiencies, others considered a massive investment in public infrastructures an absolute priority: 'Dilapidated bridges and roads, large wastewater treatment requirements, and other needs make additional public capital investment essential'.[26]

The capital needs of the developing countries, and especially of the poorest among them, have been, are, and can obviously be expected to remain huge, in a world economy that has witnessed growing inequality and in which the less affluent four-fifths of the world's population enjoy only one sixth of its income.[27] Between 1982 and 1987 the annual total net flow of foreign funds to the Third World had slipped from 116 to 97 billion dollars.[28] This decline did not reflect a reduced need for investable resources in the Third World so much as the unwillingness of international banks and markets to increase their exposure toward countries whose aggregate gross debt had

[25] See B. B. Aghevli *et al.*, *The Role of National Saving in the World Economy. Recent Trends and Prospects* (Washington: IMF, 1990).

[26] A. H. Munnel (ed.), *Is there a Shortfall in Public Investment?*, Federal Reserve Bank of Boston Conference Series no. 34 (Boston 1990), 20.

[27] United Nations, *Human Development Report 1992* (Oxford: Oxford University Press, 1992).

[28] OECD, *Financing and External Debt of Developing Countries:1988 Survey* (Paris, 1989).

reached (even excluding Eastern Europe) 850 billion dollars by the time of the 1982 debt crisis, 1.2 trillion in 1987, and nearly 1.4 trillion in 1992. Official loans came to represent the larger part of the flow of funds to the underdeveloped area, though they only partly replaced the reduced, rationed private loans. Not paradoxically, the recovery of a structural equilibrium by a number of countries, notably in Latin America, gave renewed access to international capital markets to economies that had been excluded or rationed, and thus implied renewed pressure on interest rates.

Above all, the expectation of a global excess of investment over saving was generated by the collapse of real socialism in Eastern Europe and the confidence that these planned systems would be rapidly converted into market economies. The expectation was confirmed by the flowering of estimates concerning the capital needs associated, in the short as well as the medium term, with the transition, the reconstruction, and the future development of those economies. Though differing in their assumptions and objectives, and even setting aside the special case of East Germany, these estimates envisaged annual capital flows of up to some hundreds of billions of dollars, and in any case no less than various tens of billions.[29] This prospect was seen at the same time as an opportunity to boost trade and incomes even in the industrial market economies, and especially in a strengthened Europe transformed, through the stages indicated by the 'Delors Report' (1989) and the Maastricht Treaty (1991),

---

[29] For a useful survey see S. De Nardis and S. Micossi, 'L'insufficienza del risparmio nell'economia mondiale: miti e realtà', *Luiss Quaderni di Ricerca* (1993), no. 32. In the analyses made by banks and international finance, the investment requirements in East Europe have, in effect, been considered as a possible source of pressure on saving and interest rates, together with other elements. 'Today's key fact: competition for limited global saving bred by the investment demands of German unification and Eastern Europe's liberation, the implementation of the EC's single market, the upgrading of U.S. industry, the unmet needs of Latin America, Asia, and Africa, plus the eventual restructuring of the Soviet Union and global environmental cleanup'; R. de Vries, 'Adam Smith: Managing the Global Capital of Nations', *World Financial Markets* (1990), no. 2, 2. This line of thought, widespread in international finance, is well summed up by *The Economist*: see 'Whatever Happened to Thrift?' (14 October 1989), 79; 'The Squirrels' Curse' (9 February 1991), 75; 'Bonds in Bondage' (4 May 1991), 89; and 'Eastern Europe and the World' (6 July 1991), 65.

nto an economic and monetary unit, a cohesive pole capable of managing even its relations with the East.[30]

With the major exception of East Germany, the estimated needs have remained potentialities. The Eastern European transition to capitalism has run into stronger than expected political, institutional and even socio-anthropological difficulties. This does not allow one to deny that the diffusion in the international financial market of a belief in a generalized scarcity of saving helped keep interest rates high.

[30] The dyad 'challenge/opportunity' for the European Community in the face of the events in Eastern Europe recurs, on a note of disappointed hope, in Banca d'Italia, *Relazione annuale sul 1989* (Rome, 1990).

5

Some Significant Changes in Financial Structure

The financial system is not without importance in the determination of real interest rates. Even in neo-classical theory the nature of financial institutions can influence the propensity to save and to invest as well as the net demand for money, and therefore interest rates. The effect on interest rates is nonetheless mediated. Its very sign can be appraised only on the basis of specific knowledge of or hypotheses about the values of the parameters. A more efficient and stable financial structure reduces the risks for the public and for the banks. If it reduces money demand and increases money supply, it may simultaneously reduce the propensity to save and boost the propensity to invest; consequently, the final effect on interest rates cannot be determined a priori.

In this context, deregulation—such as that which characterized financial systems, primarily that of the United States, in the 1980s—is considered a condition for allocative efficiency. Deregulation would bring the structure of interest rates, previously distorted by controls, to its highest level of 'natural' equilibrium set by productivity and thrift.[1] The increased risks of financial instability associated with deregulation, however, would push central banks toward more expansionary monetary policies, increasing expected inflation and therefore nominal, though not necessarily real, interest rates.[2]

[1] UNCTAD, *Trade and Development Report* (New York, 1991).
[2] J. Melitz and C. Bordes, 'The Macroeconomic Implications of Financial Deregulation', *European Economic Review* (1991), 155–78.

In Keynes's approach the link between interest rates and the financial structure is very different. A structure oriented more towards the markets than towards the banks, towards 'market' rather than 'customer' relationships, to institutional rather than individual investors, matters for two reasons. First, such a financial structure gives particular weight to expectations rooted in conventions. In this sense, the fertile terrain offered by finance corroborates the postulates of Keynesian theory.[3] Second, such a financial structure is particularly sensitive to uncertainty which determines the degree of confidence in the conventions. It is accordingly prone to translate the elements of political and economic uncertainty into liquidity preference, and consequently into interest rates that tend to be higher or more downwardly rigid. Obviously, these elements of uncertainty include in the first instance those that impinge specifically on the volatility of the exchange rates and of the interest rates themselves. In this perspective, the deregulation of financial systems can increase the interest rates' volatility, and therefore uncertainty, with an effect on their level. Moreover, a greater emphasis on auction markets rather than bank relations may lead to lower efficiency from the perspective of the provision of funds for the accumulation of capital—a concept central to Keynesian theory. If the transaction costs associated with auction markets are higher than those associated with banks, due to the informational advantages enjoyed by the latter, then a financial structure centred on the former produces higher long-term interest rates.[4]

---

[3] While claiming the status of 'general' theory, Keynes's analysis is undoubtedly less applicable to a manorial market or 'P.O.W. camp' economy than to a 'Wall Street' economy. See R. A. Radford, 'The Economic Organization of a P.O.W. Camp' *Economica* (1945), 189–201; and H. P. Minsky, *John Maynard Keynes* (New York: Columbia University Press, 1975). Minsky has appropriately emphasized how the theory of Keynes accords with economies in which finance is highly developed.

[4] See UNCTAD, op. cit. See also the criticism of the process of financial innovation of the 1980s by M. De Cecco, 'Financial Innovations and Monetary Theories', in M De Cecco (ed.), *Changing Money: Financial Innovation in Developed Countries* (Oxford: Blackwell, 1987). For a comparative analysis of long-term financing of firms along these lines see C. Mayer, 'New Issues in Corporate Finance', *European Economic Review* (1988), 1167–83; and M. Hellwig, 'Banking, Financial Intermediation and Corporate Finance', in A. Giovannini and C. Mayer (eds.), *European Financial Integration* (Cambridge: Cambridge University Press, 1991).

The fundamental changes in financial structures in the 1980s were broadly in line with the implicit assumptions of the Keynesian theory of interest. In domestic and international finance, the weight of markets has grown relative to that of traditional financial intermediaries; the weight of institutional investors has also grown. This transformation took place in the context of a closer, if still incomplete, integration of finance beyond national borders, akin to the archetype of a single world capital market. The uncertainty stemming from the lack of government of the world economy was thus compounded by the uncertainty stemming from the instability of exchange rates and interest rates. The environment was that of an international monetary 'non-system' in which the world's commercial and financial transactions were entrusted with far greater exchange rate flexibility than that of the previous decades.

These empirical propositions can be illustrated by a few simple indicators.

In domestic finance, between 1979–80 and the end of the 1980s the share of bank intermediaries in total financial assets fell in Germany (from 41 to 37 per cent), Canada (from 20 to 17 per cent), the United States (from 20 to 15 per cent) and especially France (from 42 to 32 per cent) and Italy (from 37 to 26 per cent); it remained stable in Japan (16–17 per cent). There was a corresponding increase in the share of financial relations established in securities markets, either directly or through non-banking intermediaries most involved in those markets. In particular, the share of non-banking intermediaries—including insurance companies and private pension funds acting as institutional investors—increased almost everywhere: from 5 to 7 per cent in Germany, from 7 to 9 in Italy, from 3 to 7 in France, from 15 to 20 in Canada, from 15 to 25 in the United States; in Japan the share remained at high levels, near 26 per cent.[5]

In international finance, with reference to gross annual flows on the world capital market, between 1981–3 and 1990–2, total bank credit grew from 87 to 109 billion dollars, but total stock

[5] See OECD, *Financial Accounts of OECD Countries*, various years.

and bond issues leapt from 69 to 276 billion.[6] From 1986 to 1991, the value of the foreign shares held by American, Japanese and European residents together grew 60 per cent to 1.3 trillion dollars, roughly half of all negotiable securities; in 1991, the share of the portfolio of the 100 largest American and European funds invested in foreign assets equalled 6 per cent (265 billion dollars) and 20 per cent (740 billion)[7] respectively. Between 1985 and 1991, the ratio of gross capital imports and exports for portfolio investments to the sum of current-account balance-of-payments receipts and disbursements roughly doubled in the United States, Japan and Germany, tripled in France, and grew ten-fold from low initial levels in Italy. The size and liquidity of the exchange markets noticeably increased: the total volume handled on the leading exchanges tripled from 1986 to 1992, reaching 880 billion dollars a day.[8]

The international economic and financial integration should have linked the real interest rates in the G-7 countries more closely with one another. Descriptive analysis does indeed show an increased convergence and correlation between domestic and foreign rates and a growing statistical influence of the world rate on national rates. Co-integration analysis has been used to test econometrically the hypothesis that capital mobility has strengthened the structural ties among national real interest rates. Keeping in mind the limitations of the method, Levy and Panetta show that a significant relation between national real rates and the G-7 average real rate does not appear in the 1960s and 1970s but it does in the 1980s, although only for the countries belonging to the European Monetary System.

Against the background of these changes in the relationship among bank intermediaries, institutional investors, and securities markets, there was a further advance in financial deepening.

---

[6] See OECD, *Financial Market Trends*, various years (for 1992, January–September; for 1981–4 only bonds). The figure does not include borrowing facilities. If these are taken into account, the total gross financing between 1985 and 1992 jumps from 281 to 610 billion dollars.

[7] Group of Ten, *International Capital Movements and Foreign Exchange Markets. A Report*, (Washington: IMF, April 1993).

[8] Ibid., 114–38.

In the 1980s, the ratio between households' net financial wealth and their disposable income remained high, near 2.5 in the United States; it grew from 1.2 to 2.2 in Japan, from 1.1 to 2 in Italy, from 1.3 to 1.9 in the United Kingdom, from 1.4 to 1.8 in Germany, from 1.5 to 1.7 in Canada and from 0.8 to 1.3 in France. In all G-7 countries, moreover, financial assets of households have increased more than real assets.[9]

Seen from the liabilities side, the growth of financial intermediation frequently appeared as a matter of speculative increases in private-sector indebtedness. This continued even after the stock market crash of October 1987, though the latter should have been a clear signal of the precariousness of the relationship between speculative purchases of shares and real estate on the one hand and heavy indebtedness at real interest rates that were also high, and showed no tendency to fall, on the other. In Japan, in the 1980s, the ratio of private-sector indebtedness to GDP rose from 1.5 to 2.2, while relative property prices tripled between 1980 and 1990, and then collapsed, and share prices quintupled between 1980 and 1989, and then collapsed. A similar cycle, albeit of lower intensity and with different timing,[10] took place in the United Kingdom and the United States. The real cost of money remained high—even higher than debtors expected for given asset prices—creating from 1989–90 a situation close to Fisher's 'debt deflation'.[11] Consumption and investment were reduced to repay debt that had become too burdensome. The correction of wealth imbalances helped aggravate the recession.

The real interest rates still vary across countries. In this respect a full international economic and financial integration has not been achieved. Real-rate convergence would require 'covered' nominal interest rates be equalized, that is the ability of capital flows to level nominal interest rates across financial instruments issued in different countries but denominated in the same

[9] A. Fazio, 'Mercati finanziari: integrazione o competizione tra settore pubblico e settore privato', *Diritto dell'economia* (1993), 301–9.

[10] For the essential data see IMF, *World Economic Outlook. Interim Assessment*, (Washington, January 1993), 33–5.

[11] I. Fisher, 'The Debt-deflation Theory of Great Depressions', *Econometrica* (1933), 337–57.

currency. This condition is not satisfied if the interest rates incorporate a risk premium related to negative features of the issuing country ('country risk'), i.e. transaction and information costs, tax burdens, actual or possible controls of capital flows, and likelihood of collapse. Equality among national real interest rates would also require a zero premium for the real and nominal exchange risk which is associated with financial instruments denominated in a currency that is different from the others.

Statistical analysis[12] suggests that in the 1980s the country risk was near zero for Germany, Japan, Canada, the United Kingdom, the United States, and fell sharply for France and Italy, especially after the liberalization of capital movements. But due to the persistence of a conspicuous, variable 'currency premium', even among these countries real interest differentials remain.

The EMS notwithstanding, the relative weight of countries with some form of fluctuating exchange rate has remained high: in terms of the dollar value of imports and exports, it equalled 55–60 per cent in June 1992 (prior to the crisis of the EMS) against 60–5 per cent in March 1979 and 15 per cent in December 1970, when the Bretton Woods system was still fully operational. For the major currencies the variability of effective nominal exchange rates has been not only greater than that which prevailed until 1971 under the Bretton Woods regime, but greater even than the already conspicuous fluctuations experienced in 1973–9 for such currencies as the dollar, the pound sterling and the yen. The variance calculated on the weekly percentage variations of the individual currencies against the dollar was often more than twice as high in 1980–3 than in 1973–9. The variability of real exchange rates also has been very high in the G-7 countries. In the 1980s, high exchange variability was frequently accompanied by high interest rate variability. Measured by the coefficient of variation, the variability of real long-term interest rates has proved equal to that of the 1970s

---

[12] J. A. Frankel, 'Measuring International Capital Mobility: A Review', *American Economic Review, Papers and Proceedings* (1992), 197–202; and De Nardis and Micossi, op. cit.

and four times higher than in the 1960s. Furthermore the variability of nominal rates has been double that of the two preceding decades.

Financial structures which become more oriented towards markets and institutional investors and interact with a world capital market that is cohesive yet segmented and exposed to high variability in interest and exchange rates lend support to a Keynesian-type explanation of the high and rigid cost of money over the last decade.

6

An Old and a New Obstacle to Lower Rates: *The Budget Deficit in the United States and the Reunification of Germany*

The American budget deficit has often been cited as an almost defining element of the Third and Fourth Conventions. It has helped to prevent the reduction in long-term real interest rates through the markets' perceptions of a bad policy mix internal and external to the United States and of a world-wide shortage of saving. It has appeared not only as a crucial determinant of the path of world interest rates over more than ten years but as a major symptom of a more general problem: the lack of consistency and the inadequacy of the mix of economic policies in governing the strategic variable represented by the cost of money.

In February 1993, immediately upon taking office, President Clinton's new Democratic Administration put forth a broad fiscal plan for the short and medium terms. In the short term, the plan aimed to stimulate the economy, in weak recovery from the recession, with public investment and tax credits to firms. These measures were expected to increase the 1993–4 budget deficit by 30 billion dollars (0.5 per cent of product) to a total of approximately 310 billions (5 per cent of product). In the medium term (1994–8), the objectives of the plan were to improve expenditure and to reduce the deficit. Expenditure for infrastructures, technology, and the environment would be increased, the public health-care system would be extended and made more efficient. Expenditures for the military and for public employment would be cut. The ratio of federal spending to total product—which increased from 21 to 24 per cent over the previous ten years, generating the deficits—would first level off and then decrease. The reduction of the deficit would also stem from an increase in tax pressure, relatively low in the United States and further lowered in the 1980s. The main components of the tax policy can be identified as the return to progressivity in income taxation, undone by the Republican Administration, and taxation of the use of energy sources.

In its short-term expansion component, the plan has immediately run up against insurmountable obstacles in Congress. The long-term restrictive component, critical to medium-run expectations, has found a good deal of support in both academic and political circles. Nonetheless, the equilibrium between fiscal rigour and redistribution of the tax burden is extremely delicate and appears hard to achieve. Only concrete movement towards it can reassure the domestic and international financial markets and remove the obstacle to lower world interest rates represented by the American structural budget deficit.

If the lead economy continues to give markets the impression that it does not save, that it prefers consumption to investment, that it drains resources from the rest of the world instead of transferring them abroad and that it is piling up debt towards future generations and foreigners, then the two conventions that came to be established and combined in the 1980s—the Third and Fourth Conventions—will continue to prevail.

The reunification of Germany (monetary on 1 July 1990, political on 3 October of that same year), following the collapse of the Berlin Wall and the breakdown of East Germany in 1989, represented an additional obstacle to a decline in the high price of money. Prior to reunification, Federal Germany enjoyed perhaps the strongest economy in the world, certainly the least beset by problems. Adequate growth, sustained accumulation of capital, competitive industries, a budget under control, relations between industry, labour, and finance tending to collusion rather than collision, low rates of monetary growth, low inflation, a strong currency, record-setting exports and trade surpluses and net credit position towards the rest of the world second only to Japan's, comprised the essential features of the West German economy when it confronted East Germany, backward and yet not small, with a population one quarter that of West Germany and an estimated output not greater than one tenth of the latter's.

The effect of reunification on the German economy and on the world economy has been interpreted as follows:

[The fall of the Berlin Wall] led quickly to the anticipation of some form of reunification of Germany, and the likely expansion of both investment and the fiscal deficit as eastern Germany would be rebuilt. During 1987–88, German long-term interest rates were about 2–3 percentage points below U.S. rates. German rates began to rise in 1989, and moved up sharply in early 1990, as the market began to see more clearly the financial implications of reunification. By mid 1990 German long-term interest rates were above U.S. rates. The DM appreciated gradually against the dollar . . . from late 1989 until early 1991, and then reversed with a gradual depreciation. The German current account moved from a surplus of nearly 5 per cent of GNP in 1989 to a small deficit in 1991. The German reunification thus provides an example of the financial markets anticipating the consequences of reasonably clear future events, bringing the future into the present. In this case German long-term bond rates rose and prices fell sharply, and the DM first appreciated against the dollar, and then reversed itself. Shifting expectations of future real fundamentals created substantial movements in current financial variables . . . When the actual expenditures began in 1991, the DM began to depreciate. Thus the combination of the rise in the German long-term rates and the path of the DM/dollar exchange rate is consistent with an anticipated fiscal and investment expansion that began to be realized in 1991.[1]

This citation from William Branson well describes the reaction of the financial markets to the reunification of Germany. But

[1] W. H. Branson, 'High world interest rates: shortage of saving or liquidity?', in P. B. Kenen *et al.* (eds.), *The International Monetary System* (Cambridge: Cambridge University Press, 1994), 123–4 and 127. Branson's interesting essay can be read in the sense that it is not the shortage of saving itself, so much as the anticipation—not necessarily 'rational' in the neo-classical sense, but reasonable in the Keynesian sense—of the shortage, that causes long-term rates to rise.

this reaction is also consistent with a deeper, less contingent interpretation that refers back to the 'German problem'.

From the economic point of view, the German problem consists in a particular form of capitalism strongly and stably based on rules of its own, that are scarcely susceptible to modification since they are the logical product of a system organized for superiority.[2] The essential features of the system and the rules that underpin it will be set out in the next section. What matters here is that reunification exacerbated the German problem and simultaneously presented Germans with the challenge of keeping their model of capitalism intact in the new situation. This challenge influenced not only Germany's economic policy but also Europe's projected monetary unification, the political purpose of which was to mitigate the German problem by placing it within the broader context of Europe. Preserving the model would entail a monetary rigour greater even than that of before the reunification; modifying it would generate uncertainty and an upward bias in interest rates.

Ex post, faced with the alternative for German society which reunification implied, the market's attitude seems to have bet on the model's preservation, following the chain of 'rational' reactions summarized by Branson, thus pushing German interest rates in an upward direction. But the market's perceptions, its reactions, and the ultimate effect on German and European interest rates appear also consistent with a different rationality, suggested by a more structural reading of the issues raised by reunification. Germany's economic policy—its budget, incomes, structural, and even its exchange rate policies—failed to show the immediate, admittedly high, flexibility demanded by reunification. The Bundesbank emphasized its hard line in defending monetary stability, the cornerstone of German capitalism. The consequences were economic recession in Germany and Europe

[2] And perhaps in order to overcome the 'fear of the world' indicated by Thomas Mann as the ultimate source in the psychology of the German people, the aggressiveness it has often manifested, and its ability to shape comprehensive, consistent systems of thought. T. Mann, *Germany and the Germans*, speech given at the Library of Congress, Washington D.C., on the occasion of Mann's 70th birthday, 1945.

as well as an identity crisis in the process of European reunification.

High interest rates pushed the German economy into its worst recession since the war. In 1993, in the West, production fell. The European economy also was dragged into recession. Even more than in the past, and in part because of the failures of other economic policies, the Bundesbank stressed the fight against inflation. Never before June 1990–August 1992 had short-term interest rates been raised even as long-term rates declined. The real long-term rate that prevailed in 1990–2 (4–5 per cent) had been matched only in periods of expansion and strong inflation (1970, 1973, 1981), and in those periods it had not remained at such levels for more than a year. Above all, the Bundesbank had never before brought real short-term rates up to near 6 per cent, with inflation and nominal (not real) long-term interest rates that were relatively low when compared to prior levels. Despite pressure from the government, the stance of monetary policy was reluctantly relaxed only after September 1992, when the growth in the money supply slowed down—approaching the ceilings—and inflation appeared likely to fall, in 1993, from 4 to 3 per cent.

Beyond the impact effects, the conversion of the devastated economy of the former DDR and its incorporation into that of Federal Germany appeared difficult and uncertain in its final outcome to German authorities and to markets. Germany's immediate economic policy response to the problems created by reunification probably contributed to the difficulties encountered by the EMS from the summer of 1992. The monetary unification of Europe was slowed down and its configuration was questioned. The system had been conceived when Germany was politically divided and free of serious economic problems. The original scheme was strained by the disequilibria connected with German reunification and its repercussions on the European economy.

These uncertainties came to represent a further obstacle to the reduction of real long-term interest rates in Europe and the world. This went beyond the recessionary pressures exerted by

Fig. 7. Short-term real interest rates in G-7 countries and Italy, 1960–1995 (quarterly figures)
Source: see the essay by Levy and Panetta in this volume.

the immediate impact of the reunification and the Bundesbank's monetary policy stance.

In 1993 *ex ante* real long-term interest rates in Germany still hovered around 3.5 per cent in the middle of a severe recession, with a decline of gross domestic product of more than 1 per cent. Such a gap between the real interest rate and the growth rate is quite unusual in Germany's post-war economy.

In an integrated capital market, in the world and in Europe, even with flexible exchange rates, a single country open to international transactions cannot usefully attempt to keep its real long-term interest rate below that prevailing abroad. There is a close analogy to the gold standard scenario recalled by Keynes ('a rate of interest lower than prevails elsewhere will be viewed with a justifiable lack of confidence'). With reference to a regime of alterable or flexible exchange rates, the monetary policy of a single country, theoretically—by money creation, inflation, and favouring investment—would be able independently to set a real interest rate below that prevailing in a 'perfect' international capital market. But if the world at large, or Europe, or Germany

Fig. 8. Long-term real interest rates in G-7 countries and Italy, 1960–1995 (quarterly figures)
Source: see the essay by Levy and Panetta in this volume.

rejects the inflation that would follow, in highly complementary economies, 'it is possible that the strategic confrontation still occurs with respect to the proper level of the real rate of interest. Again a prisoner's dilemma occurs', posing the usual choices between cooperative and non-cooperative solutions.[3]

Italy is indicative of this case. Italy emerged from the 1970s with rigid controls on capital movements and strongly negative real interest rates, approximately two points below the already very low G-7 average (Figs. 7 and 8). Faced with an inflation rate in excess of 20 per cent and an industrial sector that was slow to restructure, in 1979–80 the Bank of Italy radically altered its monetary and exchange policy in the direction of tight money and discipline through exchange rates. Real interest rates rose rapidly, especially at the short end of the spectrum. Since 1984, Italy's short-term interest rates have been on average some 2 percentage points higher than the G-7 level and systematically

---

[3] K. Hamada, 'Alternative Exchange Rate Systems and the Interdependence of Monetary Policy', in R. Z. Aliber (ed.), *National Monetary Policies and the International Financial System* (Chicago: University of Chicago Press, 1974), 29.

higher than domestic long-term rates. This stemmed from the need to maintain a restrictive monetary policy stance—given that the rate of inflation was falling, but still higher than elsewhere—and to ensure that the exchange rate would be maintained despite persistent deficits in the external current account and the removal of exchange controls.

Italy's real long-term rates were instead well below the G-7 average up to 1987. After the exchange controls were lifted,[4] the economy became much more financially open to the rest of the world. Between 1988 and 1992 Italy's gross capital movements, in both directions, exploded, from 700,000 to 2,770,000 billion lire, from 65 to 184 per cent of gross domestic product. Its foreign assets and liabilities doubled. Between 1989 and 1992, in a broad sample of Italian banks, the daily gross volume of exchange transactions grew from 15 to 22 billion dollars, with an increase near 50 per cent. The Italian economy received a radical reorientation towards full freedom of capital movements. For this reason, too, long-term interest rates have converged to the levels prevailing abroad. On average, they exceeded that level by 1 per cent up to the moment of tension in the EMS and the crisis of the lira in the summer of 1992, when real rates in Italy reached 8–10 per cent, the highest levels of the postwar

[4] Measures to restrict foreign transactions had been relied on especially after 1972. External inconvertibility of banknotes (1972), compulsory non-interest bearing deposit on overseas investments (1973), compulsory financing in foreign currency of imports (1973) and exports (1976) were the principal measures, together with recurring regulations imposing limits on advanced or deferred settlement of transactions, limited duration of accounts in foreign currency, a tax on currency sale, compulsory policy for exchange position (spot and forward) and net external position of the banks which were made subject to ceilings. In 1976, even penal sanctions were introduced for the more severe violations. Moves in the reverse direction, towards lifting controls, announced in a draft law in 1983, got under way at the end of 1984, with an initial reduction in the compulsory non-interest bearing deposit from 50 to 40–30 per cent; this was further reduced to 25–0 per cent in October 1985. Following a first attempt in 1983—among whose motivations was the need to conform with trends in the European Community— in September 1986 the government was given the go-ahead by Parliament for sweeping liberalization in the matter of exchange regulations. Under the new law, in force since 1 October 1988, while the State retains a monopoly in exchange, the general ban on transactions with abroad has been lifted and strict limits have been placed on the possibility of reintroducing exchange restrictions. The last controls were removed on 14 May 1990. Since then, for the first time in its history, Italy has operated in an exchange regime of complete freedom on an *erga omnes* basis.

era. It bears noting that the relatively high inflation rate and the accumulation of a heavy public debt could have made Italy's real long-term interest rates sensitive to high and rising exchange risks, real and nominal, already in the 1980s. This did not happen until Italy entered a phase of extreme exchange, budget, and political difficulties in June 1992.

In the long-standing debate over the real cost of money in Italy, some commentators feel that the reason why it is so high, for the state and for firms themselves, in absolute terms and as compared with other countries, must be sought in the allegedly sub-optimal management of the public debt and the inefficient bank and financial intermediation.[5] The simple data provided above may put the debate into perspective. Above all, these Italian data confirm the assumption that without controls, and quite apart from the exchange regime, a single economy, especially if beset by problems, cannot long keep its real interest rate below that of the rest of the world.

[5] At least by analogy, these controversies over the high rate of interest recall Einaudi's delightful aphorism: 'The farmers would like:

1. abundant fodder
2. dear meat
3. high-priced milk
4. abundant milk
5. abundant cheese, at high prices
6. abundant milk by-products and therefore many pigs
7. high-priced pigs

And to obtain all these contradictory things, they ask for:

8. abundant credit
9. at low cost
10. stockpiling of all sorts of goods at remunerative prices and
11. payment by somebody else' (1954).

L. Einaudi, 'Annotazioni', *Rivista del Personale della Banca d'Italia* (1974), no. 3, 13.

7

The New Rise in Interest Rates in 1994: *A Direct Comparison Between the Two Theories*

During 1993, the long-term real interest rates in the major economies fell to levels closer to the averages of the 1960s, prior to the wide fluctuation in the price of money in the final quarter of the century. The acute recession in the economies of Continental Europe and Japan, together with the ongoing expansionary trend of monetary policy in the United States, whose economy was already recovering, contributed to the downward movement of interest rates. In October 1993 the average long-term nominal rate of the G-7 touched its lowest level, 5.6 per cent. Inflation was less than 3 per cent, with a minimum of 2.1 per cent in May. According to forecasts at the end of 1993, the spread of recovery worldwide and a turnabout in the US policy towards tight money, predicted to be imminent, would not lead to a rise in long-term real rates.[1] Forecasts to 2000 indicated that inflation in G-7 would be contained and kept under control. Hence the 1993 reduction in rates was predicted to be not merely transi-

---

[1] The cyclical recovery ultimately spread from the Anglo-Saxon economies to Continental Europe. Despite persisting stagnation and financial instability in Japan, the growth rate of the G-7 gross product passed from 1.3 per cent in 1993 to a bit less than 3 per cent per year in 1994–5.

tory: the real cost of money, which had been exceptionally high for more than a decade, would once more approach the rate of growth of productive activity.

Since then, forecasts of inflation for the seven countries as a whole have remained more or less unchanged, at 3 per cent or less up to the end of the decade, and current inflation has not exceeded 2.5 per cent. But the nominal and real interest rates, as a mean for the seven countries, have risen by around two points over a twelve-month period. At the beginning of 1995 they reached, respectively, 7.5 and nearly 5 per cent, with slight downward movements in the subsequent months.

With worldwide recovery, 1994 marked a missed opportunity to relink interest rate and growth rate. In the history of long-term interest rates this year was crucial for the notable failure to govern them. Here, then, is an excellent opportunity to compare the two theories, neo-classical and Keynesian, that have hitherto been employed to account for the medium- and long-term trends of interest rates. In this chapter we shall attempt a direct comparison of the two theories, though we are aware of the difficulty of explaining the movements of real rates over so short a period of time, owing, among other things, to problems of measurement.

The spread of the cyclical recovery is not of itself sufficient to account for the rise in rates. Mitchell's pioneering empirical studies established that interest rate movements are procyclical.[2] However, the effect of the cycle has more importance for short-term rates: for long-term rates, in the typical recovery stage of a 'normal' cycle, the increase is confined within a few tenths of a percentage point,[3] a far cry from the near two percentage point increase of 1994. This sudden sharp rise in long-term real rates[4]

[2] W. C. Mitchell and A. F. Burns, *Measuring Business Cycles* (New York: NBER, 1946).

[3] R. A. Kessel, *The Cyclical Behavior of the Term Structure of Interest Rates* (New York: NBER, 1965).

[4] 'Indeed, the surge in government bond yields among the Group of Ten countries from the beginning of February through the end of March 1994 was one of the largest two-month increases recorded during the postwar period', *International Capital Markets* (Washington: IMF, September 1994), 1.

occurred in the worldwide economic framework of a cyclical recovery that was slow to spread, mild compared with previous ones and perceived by forecasters and financial markets with no little uncertainty.[5]

Why did interest rates increase beyond all expectations?

International institutions have supplied two predominant interpretations, over and above the effect of the cycle. The first of these interpretations retraces the rise in long-term rates to a *change* in basic economic variables, the so-called fundamentals; the second marks a *return* to unchanged fundamentals following an excessive downward movement in rates during 1993. Both interpretations refer to the same type of neo-classical fundamentals. They also tend to rescale the rise in real rates. This would be suggested by the return on UK index-linked government bonds, which in 1994 rose by less 1 per cent. This particular return is taken as a more reliable indicator of the base real rate of G-7 since it is 'clean', i.e. net of risk premia.[6]

Nonetheless, the suggestion that the 'clean' world real rate should be approximated with the rate expressed by the market for UK index-linked bonds is not entirely convincing. Indeed, since this market was constituted in 1981 it has come to embrace a stock of bonds worth 60 billion dollars; but it remains fairly small, even with respect to the total UK government marketable debt (15 per cent), so that yields can be influenced by the presence of a much larger non-indexed public debt. Moreover, it belongs within an economy which represents less than 6 per cent of the OECD total production and which has been subject

[5] For example, the first forecasts for 1993 made by the OECD in December 1991 indicated a 3.4 per cent growth rate for the G-7. In June 1992 the forecast had only marginally diminished to 3.1 per cent. Thereafter the estimate fell. The pessimism that began to spread at the end of 1992, on the contrary, caused the growth rate for 1994 to be underestimated, especially for Continental Europe. The underestimate was strongest in December 1993 (when the OECD predicted a growth rate for Germany and France of a mere 1 per cent, much lower than the 2.5–3 per cent that was actually achieved) and still persisted in June 1994, when the rise in long-term rates had already become a reality.

[6] See OECD, *Economic Outlook* (Paris, December 1994), 13; and European Commission, *Recent Developments in Long-term Interest Rates and their Implications*, II/618, (Brussels, December 1994), 13.

to ups and downs in its performance as well as to uncertainties in economic policy, with a high variability in 'country' risk and exchange risk. If the interest rate of a single economy is to be chosen, the Japanese rate is probably preferable. Japan's GDP is equivalent to 15 per cent of the OECD total. As far as country risk and inflation risk and expectations are concerned, the Japanese economy constantly rates near zero. In addition, the currency is strong enough to show, if anything, a tendency to exert a downward pressure on the nominal interest rates on financial assets denominated in yen. And yet, in this economy nominal long-term rates increased from 3 to 4.7 per cent in 1994. With inflation and expectations of inflation consistently nil or negative—for consumer prices and, above all, production prices—even Japanese real rates rose by nearly two points, with levels certainly well over 4 per cent, if not nearly 5 per cent.

It should be emphasized that long-term time series of interest rates—for the leading industrial economies individually and for G-7 as a whole—show movements in the real rates that, unlike the rate levels, do not change substantially according to the modality used to deflate nominal rates.

What requires to be accounted for, as stated above, is the increase by nearly two points in 1994, from 3 to 5 per cent, of the average long-term real rate in the G-7, calculated with current inflation and the 'consensus' econometric forecasts of inflation as deflators, consistently with the criterion employed for the previous sub-periods studied so far.

An increase in the world price of money as sharp as this and as concentrated in time, reaching a historically very high level, does not appear susceptible of interpretation in terms of a change in the fundamentals underpinning neo-classical theory—not confined to individual economies but extended to the industrial countries and the world economy as a whole.[7] Such an interpret-

[7] Events, even important ones, confined to single countries cannot account for a sharp, generalized contextual increase in long-term real interest rates where there are considerable differences between the main economies, e.g. in cyclical position; in inflationary expectations (perhaps growing in the USA, declining in Japan and Germany); in exchange rate trends; in the degree of complementarity of the monetary policy with other economic policies. Specific developments of the industrial economies

ation is supported by the upward trend of profit rates in the entire business sector statistically recorded in G-7 and the OECD area as a whole.[8] Yet while the rate of return on capital rose from its 1982 minimum of 12.2 per cent, in 1994 it only just exceeded that of the 1970s (15 per cent, on average), when the real rate of interest was largely negative. Moreover, the gradual increase in 1992–4—from 15.3 to 16.2 per cent—must be set against the sharp rise in the real rate of interest in 1994 and the fall, from 16 per cent to zero, in the average stock market return in the same year, which followed the increase of 1993.[9] In 1994 and 1995, the savings : income ratios of the OECD area and throughout the world—respectively one-fifth and one-quarter—far from falling, rose (by about one point in the two-year period); the rise of investment did not exceed that of savings;[10] the productivity of capital continued to sag or stagnated.[11]

According to the second interpretation mentioned above, the fundamentals showed no alteration as a whole, but the rise in interest rates marked a return of the world price of money to the highest values corresponding to the neo-classical fundamentals, which it had diverged from previously. In this interpretation, the

in 1994 could be interpreted as change in 'fundamentals': the bull rally on the Tokyo Stock Exchange in the first half of 1994; the unexpectedly rapid expansion of the money stock in Germany in the first months of that year; the uncertainties in politics and public finance in Italy, Canada and Sweden; the high quotation of securities on the capital markets of emerging economies, like those of Central and South America. Certain of these phenomena, however, have subsequently been attenuated or reversed. Above all, they may serve to explain not so much an upward movement of the long-term real rate on a world scale as variations in the differentials among the interest rates in the different countries.

[8] OECD, *Economic Outlook* (Paris, June 1995), Table 25, p. A28.

[9] T. Helbling and R. Wescott ['The Global Real Interest Rate', Staff Studies for the *World Economic Outlook* (Washington D.C., September 1995)] kindly supplied the 1994 data of the average stock market return for the industrialized countries.

[10] For provisional estimates of saving and investment in 1994–5, see IMF, *World Economic Outlook* (May 1995), Table A44, 188. There is a glaring contrast between the neo-classical hypothesis and the positive correlation of long-term real rates and the *ex post* international propensity to save, observed since 1988, with the two variables which show a declining trend up to 1993 and an increase in 1994. At the world level, *ex post*, saving and investment do not coincide, due to significant 'errors and omissions' in the statistics.

[11] OECD, *Economic Outlook* (various years); and IMF, *World Economic Outlook*, cit., 32 ('Capital Formation and Employment').

rise would have had a 'corrective' effect on the excessively low levels of rates resulting from a speculative bubble which led to mispricing in 1993. In 1993, new and poorly informed investors made purchases on the international securities market, facilitated by mutual funds and driven by the unsatisfactory returns on bank savings deposits. Large investors—like non-financial companies and local administrations in the United States—became over-exposed on those markets and subsequently registered serious capital losses. The downward pressure, followed by the upward pressure, on long-term interest rates was transformed into a bubble by heavily-indebted speculators, like the 'hedge funds'.

The weakness of this interpretation lies not so much in the difficulty of evaluating the novelty and the weight of investment decisions as in its basic assumption: namely, that real rates in 1993 were particularly low with respect to the level justified by the fundamentals.

The 1993 real rate of 3 per cent in G-7 appears higher, with respect not only to the 1970s but even to the 1950s and 1960s. At that time, the real rates averaged around 2 per cent, with very high annual growth rates of production (5 per cent) and mild inflation rates of consumer prices (less than 4 per cent). In 1993 the real rate of interest exceeded the rate of growth, current and expected in the short term, not only of real GDP but also of potential output. This in a cyclical situation that in Japan and continental Europe continued to be one of serious recession, with a wide gap between effective and potential production. On the basis of deviations of GDP from trend, four points of cyclical trough can be identified for G-7 as a whole: at the end of 1962, at the end of 1970, at the beginning of 1975 and at the end of 1982. In the first two shorter, less-intense cycles, when the trough was reached real interest rates were, respectively, 1.9 and 1.5 per cent; in the most acute phase of the recession following the first oil crisis, the real rates were negative (–3.6 per cent); at the end of 1982 they stood at 5 per cent. The recessions of 1974–5 and 1981–2 stemmed from supply shocks. The first oil crisis was confronted with accommodating economic policies and real rates fell to negative values; on the contrary, the second shock was followed by restrictive policies (and an abrupt change in policy mix, especially in the United States and Italy) which provoked a dramatic surge in rates. The first two episodes—1962 and 1970—were therefore more similar to the most recent recession. With respect to these, the levels of the real rates in 1992—cyclical minimum for G-7—appear decidedly higher (4–5 per cent). If the level at 1993 end (3 per cent) is compared with those—cyclically comparable, at one year from the minimum point of the recession—at 1963 end (around 2 per cent) and 1971 (again 2 per cent), the result of the comparison is confirmed: and this in spite of the fall in real rates in 1993, one year after the cyclical inversion of productive activity in G-7. In 1993 the drop in nominal interest rates shaved only a little over half a point off the real rates in G-7. The level of real rates remained high, especially in the countries still in recession. Measured in terms of production prices, in order to assess the burden on firms undergoing severe recession and involved in restructuring their production, the level is considerably higher.

In fact, the level of real rates in a year of serious recession was still high as against both the long-term trends and the values recorded in similar stages of the cycle. Above all, as seen in Chapter 2, the neo-classical fundamentals fail to explain why interest rates were persistently high prior to 1993 and thus to specify the starting point of the supposed bubble.

On the contrary, the movements in interest rates in 1993–5 can be read in line with the Keynesian view.

As we saw in the previous chapter, the premise is that the world real interest rate is determined in a financial market which is itself worldwide: not yet a 'single' market, but already a tightly-integrated one operating 24 hours a day, and highly self-referential and speculative in Keynes's sense. This market can be described in the words of James Tobin who, like Keynes in 1936, has since 1978 been suggesting that its excesses be curbed: 'In today's world of high capital mobility . . . if currencies are floating, they can fluctuate widely. If the authorities attempt to peg them, the costs of doing so, measured by reserve losses or interest-rate increase, can be extremely high . . . defeated . . . by rational and self-fulfilling attacks'.[12]

Unlike the interpretation based on the formation of a bubble, the Keynesian reading rests on the evidence that in 1993 the markets judged interest rates to be too high. This took place on the wave of a US monetary policy that was still expansionary—and which the markets supported by reducing returns on bonds—and, above all, in relation to the European situation, where the markets promoted a fall in rates. The fall of interest rates in Europe followed the break-up of the ERM. It led to an easing of monetary conditions, first in the countries that had devalued or had allowed their currencies to fluctuate, and subsequently in those that had remained in the ERM with wider bands of fluctuation. The expansionary stance taken by Germany's monetary policy, though still cautious, likewise contributed. But the decisive element was the perception by financial markets of the contrast between the high level of rates in the European economies—still in recession, like Japan's economy—and the lower level in the US economy, where the recovery had already started. The lag in the fall in European rates promised capital gains on investments in European bonds. The portfolio allocation of US institutional investors consistent with this perspective favoured the fall in European long-term rates. The movement went beyond what was deemed advisable by the

[12] 'The same interest arbitrage that limits the autonomy of a central bank in a fixed-exchange-rate regime restricts its powers under floating. If similar financial assets denominated in different currencies are perfect substitutes in private portfolios, they cannot bear different interest returns in their domestic currencies unless those differences are offset by expected exchange rate movements. Central banks and governments cannot always create exchange rate expectations consistent with the domestic interest rates they desire.' And again: 'Outcomes of financial markets impinge on real economies, local, national, and international, where adjustments are sluggish, transactions are costly, transportation is slow and expensive, substitutions are imperfect and time-consuming, and expectations are fuzzy.' B. Eichengreen, J. Tobin, and C. Wyplosz, 'Two Cases for Sand in the Wheels of International Finance', *Economic Journal* (1995), 162–72. Tobin's proposal, now more than formerly, is for a 'transaction tax on purchases and sales of foreign exchange.' The real alternative, total or partial, is firmer government of the world economy, which the markets will perceive as such.

Bundesbank in its reduction of short-term rates, carefully attuned to the inflation trend. The Bundesbank changed its policy stance as soon as the fall of inflation showed signs of halting. Hence it was international investors, rather than the central banks, who acted to resolve the inconsistency represented by the high price of money.

The fall in real rates did not bring their level below a relatively high floor. From that level they rose rapidly when the expectation of a further fall began to lose weight. The turnabout got under way in the autumn of 1993 in the United States. As the US recovery gathered strength, with low short-term rates, markets became convinced that a reversion by the Federal Reserve to a tight money policy was imminent. 'Future' rates on the US money market took this change for granted. Long-term spot rates came into line, recording an increase by some 50 basis points in 10-year returns in the last quarter of 1993. Following this rise, the US securities market stabilized at the end of the year. Many long, highly-leveraged positions remained open. In the same period, the German 10-year rates were still diminishing and fell below the US levels.

The Federal Reserve's decision, on 4 February 1994, to raise the rate on Federal Funds by one quarter of one point produced a violent reaction in the markets. This had two distressing effects: it led US 10-year rates to increase by more than half a point, and it involved the rates of all the major countries in this increase, beginning with Germany. As compared to the increases in short-term rates in the United States at the end of 1982 and 1986, in this recent episode the long-term rates rose earlier and higher than the short-term ones in the United States itself. Elsewhere, the increase followed hard on the heels of the US rise, whereas domestic short-term rates were steady or diminishing. Correlations between US long-term rates on the one hand, and those of the other major countries on the other, were almost equal to one in 1994, which had never previously been the case.

The repercussion of the Federal Reserve's move on the US securities market has been ascribed by some to the fact that it signalled an inflation risk that financial operators were not fully aware of; others attribute it to the fact that the intervention by the central bank was, on the contrary, too limited in its scope to allay the market's already rooted apprehension of a return of inflation. But the first interpretation ignores the fact that intervention had for some time been expected and was indeed taken for granted: it was thus hardly sufficient to alter the market's perspective of the fundamentals. Rather, the intervention by the Federal Reserve confirmed the inflationary fears of the market, but owing to its limited scope it failed to reduce them. In particular, it seemed insufficient *vis-à-vis* the large number of investors with very risky long-term positions, the maintenance of which implied a high degree of confidence. There is evidence that the previous growth in the investments by the 'hedge funds' worsened the effects of the Federal Reserve's manœuvre. The negative response by the market was reflected in other signals indicative of ongoing friction between the Federal Reserve and the Administration over the restrictive character of the former's monetary policy. And once again there loomed the possibility, subsequently to become a reality, that the United States might consider employing the depreciation of the dollar against the yen as a weapon in its trade conflict with Japan. In the latter country, likewise, expectations of further reductions in rates were dimmed by developments in the domestic financial market.[13]

By contrast, in view of the rise in the German rates, it is necessary to account for the decline in the expectation that Europe would reproduce the experience of the United States, with a fall in interest rates protracted until recovery had been accomplished. At the start of the year, this expectation led international analysts to predict a reduction in German rates and a strengthening of the dollar against the DM. It was held likely,

---

[13] 'Prospects for further interest rate declines in Japan were dampened when Japanese equity prices proved to be more buoyant than expected and when reports surfaced that certain Japanese Government Trust accounts would switch from being net purchasers to become net sellers of Japanese Government Bonds (JGBs); yields on ten-year JGBs rose sharply in January.' IMF, *International Capital Markets*, cit., 4.

if not certain, that the German rates—and thus those of continental Europe, where the cyclical recovery seemed uncertain
and in need of support—would be decoupled from the US rates.

In the upsurge of long-term rates in Germany that followed
the Federal Reserve's manœuvre, disinvestment in German securities played a role in covering the losses sustained in specu-
lation on US securities. At the new level of rates the decoupling
required heavier involvement on the part of the Bundesbank.
The risk of an acceleration of the money supply in Germany
induced the Bundesbank not to reduce the official rates on 17
February. In the evaluation of the markets, the reduction of
Germany's official rates would have been in contrast to a
German inflation that continued to be higher than the target set
by the central bank, with too rapid an increase in monetary
aggregates and with signs of recovery in the German economy.
The increase in German long-term rates followed that of the US
rates. The Bundesbank in April and May obtained a temporary
decoupling through two additional expansionary manœuvres
that ran counter to the Federal Reserve's restrictive ones. Thereafter, the German central bank no longer felt it necessary to
intervene, even in the face of the two upsurges in long-term rates
that occurred in June and early autumn. Even faced with
increases in the real rates that were perhaps unwelcome, the
Bundesbank seemed to doubt the efficacy of any further intervention, seeing that the markets had by now become sceptical
as to the possibility of decoupling the European and US rates.
The Federal Reserve, on the contrary, intensified its restrictive
policy by repeatedly raising official rates and rates on federal
funds. But not until the summer did it manage to halt the rise of
long-term rates and only at the end of the year, following mid-
November's stronger dose of monetary tightening, was it able to
bring about a mild inversion.

The liquidation of long positions on bonds was intensified
and accelerated by operations and technical conditions that
spread through the financial markets. These include the following: the pre-established limits for sustainable loss that trip off a
planned, automatic selling mechanism; the reduced margin of

accountable losses in the first months of 1994, due to the profits realized in 1993; the still fairly low liquidity of the European bond markets as compared to the US ones; and the high degree of indebtedness and limited capital base underpinning the long-term positions of many operators.

At the end of 1994, 10-year US and German rates were 2 percentage points higher than at the beginning of the year, with an inflation rate substantially unaltered in the United States and down by 0.7 per cent in Germany. The rise in real rates almost covered the growth in GDP forecast for the two countries in 1995.

The different strategies pursued by the US and German central banks proved unable to curb the rise in long-term rates. The first, by means of continual intervention, aimed to curb market expectations; the second elected not to follow these expectations in order to influence them but rather to contrast them by indicating its intention to maintain a firm monetary stance.

Seldom before has the market, with its conventions, brought influence to bear on the central banks as it did during the fluctuation of interest rates in the period 1993–4. Far from following the line of central banks, the market obstructed their intentions and manœuvres, with small regard for differences in the business cycle and in inflation. Various observers have noted that in this way governments are surrendering their capacity to influence the economy to the domestic and international financial markets, which are closely integrated.

At their periodic international summits, the governments of the major countries have voiced their concern over the difficulty of guiding interest rates and over the high and increasing level of these rates in 1994. The representatives of the G-7 countries do not share the view that the market would be more capable than the central banks of tackling inflation, financial instability, and unemployment. Yet the conviction that the political government of the economy is more effective than guidance stemming *ex post* from the mutable opinions of the financial market has not been translated into effective action. It has failed to lead those countries which determine the fate of the world economy to tighten the coordination of their policies. This would be the right attitude to take towards a global market playing its games with not one single central bank but a number of central banks which find it increasingly hard to maintain their status at international level.

Since the early 1980s, what we identified as the Third Convention has shown no sign of fading but has indeed gathered new strength and once again manifested itself in an upward pressure on interest rates.

This is a consequence of the failure to satisfy the need for coordination. Given the purpose of achieving a reduction of real rates and their diversification among countries, in an international financial market such as we have described this need had become more urgent owing to a number of factors. It was necessary to encourage international recovery by governing, more than previously, the differences in cyclical conditions among the major economies. These differences were not merely important in themselves but were in flat contrast with the re-equilibrium of the balances of payments and the net financial standing with other countries. The recovery was led by the United States, the world's largest debtor, under a chronic current account deficit; whereas Japan, the leading creditor and surplus country, found it hard to emerge from the recession. Hence the disequilibria in foreign accounts tended to increase. Likewise, it was feared that unless exchange variations were regulated, they could cause conflict between domestic and foreign equilibrium in the major economies. And most importantly, while the appreciation of the yen against the dollar was of use in reducing the trade deficit of the United States with Japan, it interfered with the recovery of the Japanese economy and so with the growth of the world economy as a whole.

The closer coordination necessitated by this situation has run up against at least four obstacles:

(1) Among the policy makers there has been an insufficient convergence of opinion in the analysis of the causes underlying the upsurge of interest rates, in evaluating the levels reached by real rates and in viewing the 'high' long-term real rate as a

problem demanding urgent attention. Neo-classical-type interpretations have prevailed.[14] But these viewpoints, in turn, are
divided in ascribing the *ex ante* shock to the propensity to save
and to the propensity to invest, with uncertain negative repercussions on economic growth. The negative consequences would
take shape if saving decreases, but not if investment prospects
improve.[15] The anti-inflationary commitment of the central
banks has been stressed, intensified, and rendered more urgent
Central banks have managed to curb the increase of real rates
but only as regards the component attributable to the risk that
inflation might exceed the levels expected by the market. Yet the
central banks of the major countries have not openly declared,
nor made clear to the markets, their profound unease about the
levels of the long-term real rate; this unease exists independently of the effective ability of central banks to reduce rates by
broad-based monetary policies or by variations in the short-term
rates, downwards or upwards as circumstances require. The
countries with the highest public or foreign debts declared
greater commitment to addressing the problem of high interest
rates; but their appeals were suspected of opportunism and were
answered with the invitation to 'put their house in order'.

(2) The markets perceived a conflict of opinion among the
major countries also regarding the exchange rates. Though rarely
proclaiming themselves as such, two distinct schools of thought
emerged.[16] The first, the 'activist' approach, advised graduating
monetary policy and short-term rates as a function of desirable
exchange rates aiming at external and domestic equilibrium; in
addition, the buying and the selling of currency by the central
banks was felt to be useful, or at least supportive of the appropriate interest rates differentials between the short-term interest
rates. The second, by contrast, held that each country should

[14] See IMF, *World Economic Outlook*, cit., especially ch. 5.
[15] 'If high nominal rates reflect an increase in the rate of return, high nominal interest
rates are not detrimental to growth'. European Commission, *Recent Developments in
Long-term Interest Rates*, cit., 18.
[16] See P. Clark *et al.*, *Exchange Rates and Economic Fundamentals* (Washington:
IMF, 1994); and M. Mussa *et al.*, *Improving the International Monetary System*
(Washington: IMF, 1994).

concentrate on pursuing 'optimal' economic policies targeted on domestic equilibrium, relying on the efficiency of the exchange market to identify the exchange rates most suitable for external equilibrium. In the view of the markets, Japan answered most nearly to the first requirement, Germany to the second, while the United States took a more ambiguous position. On the markets, exchange rates showed clear misalignment and sharp variability. Regarding 'real' exchange rates, the yen climbed beyond all previous maximum values, with strong deflationary pressure on the tradable goods produced by Japan; the DM returned to the highest levels that it had touched briefly only in the early 1970s; by contrast, the dollar frequently threatened to sink below its historical minimum values; and Italian and Swedish currencies fell and remained at the lowest levels since 1973. Regarding the volatility of exchanges, the oscillations in nominal effective rates of European currencies and in bilateral rates against the DM were comparable to the widest variations, recorded in the last twenty years, in a period of downward convergence of inflation and cyclical alignment of most economies; the DM and the yen saw no reduction in the high variability prevailing since the 1970s, both with respect to the US dollar and in their bilateral relations.

(3) Although the Uruguay Round was approved at the end of 1993, commercial friction once more became acute, especially between the United States and Japan: 'The intensification of the trade dispute between the United States and Japan—in mid-February and again in early March—was seemingly read by the market as a signal that the U.S. authorities would be more inclined to tolerate a higher yen as a mechanism for inducing Japan either to implement greater macroeconomic stimulus (than proposed hitherto) or to grant greater market-access concessions'.[17] Some 40 per cent of the US trade deficit, which reached 166 billion dollars in 1994, stemmed from trade with Japan. The automobile sector accounts for more than 50 per cent

[17] IMF, *International Capital Markets*, cit., 4. On the developments in world trade in these last years see N. Kirmani *et al.*, *International Trade Policies. The Uruguay Round and Beyond* (Washington: IMF, 1994).

of the commercial imbalance between the two countries: along with consumer goods, this is the sector in which the competitiveness of US industry witnessed the most serious decline during the 1980s. On the other hand, the United States is the world's major exporter of services and records substantial and increasing surplus in this item of the balance of payments: about 15 billion of the 60 billion surplus achieved in 1994 derives from trade with Japan, which is a net importer of services. In the automobile and parts sector, the United States in 1994 put further pressure on Japan to increase its imports. However, no agreement was reached.[18]

(4) Within the major countries, insufficient progress has been made in the mix of economic policies, notably in the combination of fiscal and monetary policy. There has certainly been less progress than would be feasible with the onset of recovery and a renewed prospect of growth. According to the estimates of the International Monetary Fund for the G-7 as a whole, the reduction in public deficit between 1993 and 1995 was scanty: from 4.1 to 3.2 per cent of GDP and only from 2.9 to 2.5 per cent in the structural components of public expenditure, allowing for the effect of the cyclical recovery. According to OECD estimates, the primary deficit—the deficit net of interest payments—fell from 1.3 to 0.1 per cent. With interest rates nearly double growth rates, this is too little to prevent a further rise in the ratio of public debt to GDP; and it has indeed risen from 68 to 72 per cent. Plans for fiscal consolidation in the medium term have been judged as generally inadequate by the financial markets. This is even true of the United States, despite the progress it has made in restoring balance to public finance.[19]

[18] Bilateral negotiations in five other sectors, mostly regarding exchange of services, have been more successful.

[19] 'The August 1993 budget legislation, the robust economic expansion, and net sales of assets of failed thrift institutions have helped reduce the deficit of the federal government on a unified basis. However, the administration's February budget proposal implies little further progress toward deficit reduction in the foreseeable future. The staff's projections suggest that the federal deficit and the debt-to-GDP ratio will begin to rise again after FY 1995. Even assuming that effective measures to curtail health care costs and other entitlements are adopted, it would be difficult to achieve the necessary further improvement in the fiscal balance in the medium term. Fiscal policy should

Between 1993 and 1995, the US public deficit is estimated to have fallen from 3.4 to around 2 per cent of output, but only from 3 to 2.4 per cent allowing for the cycle. The persistence of an imbalance of public finance in the world's major economy and in the G-7 countries as a whole has two negative implications. It is feared that the economic policies underpinning expectations of a fairly low inflation in the future will remain unimplemented. Secondly, monetary policies may continue to be 'overburdened'. They would thus be less safe in Keynes's sense, and so less able to influence long-term rates. Economic studies based on non-Keynesian theory have found a close positive correlation, with reference to the 1980s and 1990s, between the public deficits or debts and the real—more often short-term—interest rates in the industrial countries.[20] The prevailing interpretation has been that the deficits on current account in the public sector—implying a smaller build-up of saving in view of the only partial compensation (around 50 per cent) offered by increased private saving—and the public debts—implying a larger offer of bonds and an increased demand for loanable funds—would cause a mechanical upward pressure on interest rates ('crowding out'). But the correlation between public finance and interest rates can also be viewed in a quite different, Keynesian perspective. As well as creating uncertainty and concern *per se*, the precarious, if not worsening, situation of public finance invests the financial market with the fear that the monetary policy is not supported by the budgetary policy and is thus neither safe nor credible. The negative repercussions of an

focus on measures to contain the growth of spending, and also on measures to raise federal revenues as expenditure restraint alone is unlikely to bring about the needed consolidation. The relatively low saving rate in the United States underscores the need for strengthened efforts at fiscal consolidation so that the burden of adjustment of the external imbalance does not fall on investment.' IMF, *World Economic Outlook*, cit., 23–4.

[20] T. Helbling and R. Wescott, op. cit. Following a different, though still non-Keynesian, approach the correlation between public debt and real rate of interest has also been found by E. S. Phelps, *Structural Slumps. The Modern Equilibrium Theory of Unemployment, Interest, and Assets* (Cambridge, Mass.: Harvard University Press, 1994), ch. 17. Phelps analyses a variety of channels, in addition to the nature and intensity of capital accumulation, through which a 'high' real interest rate depresses employment.

upsurge in interest rates are manifested through an increased demand for money rather than through the increased offer of government bonds.

The four obstacles we have described have adversely affected the degree of coordination of economic policies and of cohesion in governing the world economy. The progress needed has certainly not been forthcoming. Hence, the attempt in 1994 to coordinate at least the monetary policies—tighter in the United States, easier in Germany and Japan—failed to persuade the financial markets to accept a lower worldwide long-term real rate of interest.

Incapable of expressing an international policy that should guide and orient world finance, the governments of the three major countries have ultimately highlighted the interpretations of interest rates set forth by the neo-classical stance, even in the face of shifts and upheavals in the capital markets as considerable as those of 1993–5. In the Keynesian reading we propose, this reliance on the fundamentals of parsimony and productivity looks very much like escapism. The markets, with keener insight than the neo-classical reasoning, evidently see as the real 'fundamental' the weak government of the world economy.

8

Beyond the 'Conventions'

The will and the ability to govern the world economy depend on the way the stance of economic policy is coordinated, notably among the three major economies of the United States, Germany and Japan. They depend therefore on the policy mix, understood both as a combination of the instruments of the national economic policies and as a blend of their individual approaches. But these countries represent three forms of capitalism, three different 'capitalisms'. They differ in the role of government, the mode of organizing firms and labour, the extent of specialization in production, the degree of international openness, the structure of the financial system, the relations between banks and industry, and the aversion to inflation. The differences in policy stance and instruments are therefore deeply rooted, because they are congenital and not tied only to leads and lags in the business cycle.

Underlining these specific features brings out the difficulties in coordinating policies and avoids false hopes of easily lowering the cost of money: those difficulties are a source of uncertainty in themselves, and thus a creeping factor of downward rigidity of interest rates in a world with a high degree of financial integration. But it also enables one to appreciate the range of possibilities available to govern the world economy—a range that is limited, though not nullified, by the ways in which the economic policies of America, Japan and Germany are influenced by the specific features of their economies.

The literature on 'capitalisms' allows us to use their features to evaluate the hypothetical flexibility of economic policy in each of the three countries suggested by historical experience. The resulting scale sees the policy emerging from American capitalism as the most flexible; that of German capitalism as the least flexible; and in an intermediate and in some ways ambiguous position, that of Japanese capitalism.

The flexibility of American economic policy historically derives from the fact that American capitalism probably represents the purest expression of an *adaptive society*.[1] This is shown by the acceptance of the sovereignty of private enterprise and the subordinate role of state intervention as facts of nature.[2] The function of the State is carefully fragmented and distributed according to the principle of *countervailing powers*[3] and it is always open to the influence of interest groups. Economic development and its accompanying changes are not therefore directed by the State but rather they are company-led.[4] Control of the management of firms is largely entrusted to the capital market. The latter must be left as free as possible to express itself through auction-determined prices or interest rates. The management of the economy has therefore drawn flexibility from the capacity of politics to govern the State, adjusting to new situations by filtering the pressures of the various social groups. The market becomes the principal regulator of the triangular relations among firms, labour and finance. This flexibility renders acceptable a high variability in the rates of inflation, unemployment, and interest. But precisely because it derives from a particular openness to new demands, it introduces a variability that strongly prejudices the management of the world economy, given the enormous political and economic weight of the United States.

In the United States economic policy has had to come to grips with the persistence of the budget deficit. The US budget deficit constitutes an essential component of the Third and Fourth

---

[1] H. Stein, 'The Triumph of the Adaptive Society', *The American Economist* (1990), 5–21.

[2] A. Shonfield, *Modern Capitalism* (London: Oxford University Press, 1965).

[3] J. K. Galbraith, *American Capitalism. The Concept of Countervailing Power* (Boston: Houghton Mifflin, 1952).

[4] J. Zysman, *Governments, Markets, and Growth* (Oxford: Robertson, 1983), 92.

Conventions that have contributed over these last years to the downward rigidity of real interest rates.

Long neglected in the 1980s, the budget problem endures, despite the reduction of the deficit in recent years. This can only cause unease. And yet, today more than in the past, budget deficits and public expenditure do not appear to be integral nor in any way necessary to the *modus operandi* of American capitalism: from this perspective, it should be possible to address them. The problem seems to lie in the obvious reluctance of any society to accept an increase in taxation. Yet in the United States taxation is particularly low: 30 per cent of product, against an average of over 40 per cent in the rest of the OECD. Household saving is also particularly low: 5 per cent of disposable income, against an average of 12 per cent in the rest of the OECD area. Both the renewed proof of the adaptability of the American economy and the equilibria of the world economy depend on the capacity to raise these two rates to something closer to world averages.

German capitalism is firmly based on a model of organized private enterprise with high concentration of power.[5] Its salient features are on the one hand the special relationship between universal banks and firms through which finance controls industry, and on the other the special importance of monetary policy in the system of industrial relations. The first element is based on the banks' capacity to maintain stable long-term relationships in the financing of firms. It requires low inflation and stable long-term interest rates.[6] But it also involves holding the real interest rate at a high average level: this may be seen as a stimulus to efficiency for an industrial complex that is shielded from competition 'from below' precisely by its ties to the banks. The second element emerges from the fact that a monetary policy that never accommodates inflation is an integral part of German-style incomes policy. When contracts are up for re-

[5] Shonfield, op. cit.

[6] G. Nardozzi, *Tre sistemi creditizi* (Bologna: Il Mulino, 1983), and 'Structural Trends of Financial Systems and Capital Accumulation: France, Germany, Italy', Commission of the European Community, Directorate-general for Economic and Financial Affairs, *Economic Papers* (Brussels, 1983), no. 14.

newal, the central bank's unwavering commitment to a stable or appreciating exchange induces the unions to measure the effects of wage demands directly on the competitiveness of exports and on employment.[7]

The monetary policy of the Deutsche Bundesbank is thus the complement to the dialectic between finance and industry, as well as between capital and labour. It is a mainstay of the economic policy of a state that seeks not to guide development but to maintain the conditions that ensure that development is 'negotiated'[8] within the relationship between financial and industrial capital, an historically enduring feature of the German system. Hence economic policy is structurally not very flexible. It seems to follow the tenets of Fisherian theory with the real interest rate tending to a stable natural equilibrium. The nominal rate includes the rate of inflation perceived by the financial markets, held down in Germany by a monetary policy that is both strict and, not by chance, essentially monetarist.

Japanese capitalism is also highly structured in a model with concentration of power. Unlike the German economy, however, it contains strong elements of 'planning'. The financial system is based on the banks' strong ability to control firms even in the presence of a vast market for capital, and is used as an essential tool to sustain and direct economic growth. The administration of financial flows tends to maintain interest rates at relatively low levels.[9] This seems to be the main element of rigidity in Japan's economic policy. On the other hand, Japan's policy, unlike Germany's, has shown great flexibility in repeatedly altering its development strategy as historical conditions evolved. Thanks also to the Maekawa Report, the nature of the economic problem of Japan should be fairly clear, to Japanese economists, politicians, and commentators. It consists in redirecting growth from an export-led process to one centred on private consumption and public expenditure, aimed at a greater satisfaction of individual and social needs. These needs have been contained,

---

[7] D. Soskice, 'Wage Determination: the Changing Role of Institutions in Advanced Industrialized Countries', *Oxford Review of Economic Policy* (1990), 36–61.

[8] Zysman, op. cit., 92.   [9] Ibid.

subordinated to a straightforward maximization of growth, with low wages and low private and public consumption; in fact, they have been contained so much and for so long that the citizenry has almost lost sight of the ultimate reason for the enormous national effort to compete and produce with efficiency.

Michio Morishima, recalling Max Weber, has brought to our attention the potentially decisive nature of Japan's cultural element if the country is to succeed in this coming transformation. This is the same element that raised Japan, over little more than a century, to the rank of an economic superpower:

Japan . . . possessed only this first kind of religion (an ideology providing religious justification for the position of those in power and upholding the *status quo*) and lacked any religion of the second type (a religion founded on the basis of individuals with the aim of helping humanity). As a result neither individualism nor internationalism developed and the people had no religion of their own, having become completely non-religious . . . Since this areligiousness of the Japanese people led them to become materialistic, and since they were at the same time on the other hand also nationalistic, they had no hesitation in working together for the material prosperity of Japan as a nation.[10]

The strong element of synthesis in Japanese society must now be tempered in a society less holistic and more respectful of the needs of the individual.[11] That is, it must be confirmed in its guiding role to defeat those vested interests—namely, in agriculture, real estate and services—which would suffer from a change in the growth model and which have so far resisted such a change.[12] The relationship between economic policy, the

[10] M. Morishima, *Why has Japan 'Succeeded'? Western Technology and the Japanese Ethos* (Cambridge: Cambridge University Press, 1982), 196; see also S. Tsuru, *Japan's Capitalism* (Cambridge: Cambridge University Press, 1993).

[11] 'In the holistic conception the needs of the individual are ignored or subordinated; in the individualistic conception the needs of society are ignored or subordinated.' L. Dumont, *Homo aequalis: genesi e trionfo dell'ideologia economica* (Milan: Adelphi, 1984), 18 (original edn. *Homo aequalis. Genèse et épanouissement de l'idéologie économique,* Paris: Gallimard, 1977).

[12] In February 1988, Haruo Maekawa explained with courteous clarity to one of the present authors that his plan was exposed to the obstacles raised by the vested interests it threatened in the same measure as it was necessary for the well-being of Japan and of the world.

economy, and foreign policy naturally adds further complexity to the commitment to change that Japan has to meet.[13]

The history we have reconstructed and sought to interpret here illustrates that the path of interest rates has been determined by the result of a double confrontation: the confrontation at the summit meetings of the leading countries regarding the economic policies of the three capitalisms, and the confrontation between the policy line expressed by those *fora* and a world financial system that is ever more integrated and market-oriented. In the first instance, initiatives have had to come from the United States. This occurred both with the reversal of monetary policy in October 1979, which set off one of the most restrictive operations in history, and with the opposite reversal in 1989, which began one of the most prolonged phases of monetary expansion. On the other hand, at least over the last two decades, there have been no visible redirections in German monetary policy. Japanese policy seems to adapt itself to the events and conditions created by America's economic policy. In the second confrontation, the growing weight of the markets and of the short-term calculus of the 'fluid' investor have contributed to the downward rigidity of interest rates. This was particularly evident when the expansionary stance of American monetary policy, not seconded by its German counterpart, proved to be less effective than expected.

[13] See A. Morita, *Made in Japan* (New York: Weatherhill, 1987); and S. Ishihara, *The Japan that Can Say No* (New York: Simon and Schuster, 1989).

9

We Are Not Condemned . . .

The analysis developed above reproposes Keynes's conception of the rate of interest as a conventional phenomenon through a critical review of neo-classical interpretations and a reading of the essential economic facts of the last twenty years. The conventions, like those we have identified in the main events of the world economy, are the expression not of necessity but of freedom.[1] This freedom corresponds to the will to steer the economy by using economic policy and to the capacity to affirm this will, especially since financial markets operate with a basic asymmetry: they push the long-term interest rate upward when the monetary authorities tend in that direction or when uncertainty increases; and they resist lower rates when the economic policy that seeks to reduce them is not considered sufficiently determined, realistic, or internally consistent.

The obstacles that have impeded a management of the world economy capable of inducing the financial markets to accept a prudent but significant reduction in long-term interest rates are objective and not merely of an economic nature. They are rooted in the characteristics that define societies like those of the United States, Germany and Japan. The differences in the structure of the leading economies render the coordination of economic policies and its perception by financial markets more necessary and more difficult.

In the Keynesian conception the high price of money is a matter of economic policy and not, as neo-classical doctrine would have it, the necessary result of a calculation prefigured by

[1] J. Robinson, *Freedom and Necessity. An Introduction to the Study of Society* (London: Allen & Unwin, 1970).

the theory itself. We have stressed, following Keynes, the absolute urgency of a consistent, convincing policy line in the management of the world economy. This is essential to the loosening of the constraint imposed by interest rates that are conventionally 'high'. It is essential, even considered apart from the various specific contents given to economic policy in the particular circumstances of the major countries.

Suitable economic policies can be and have been designed; they also emerge implicitly from an examination of the failures and omissions of economic policy as pursued by the major countries over the last fifteen years. We are not condemned to the perpetuation of the high interest rates which the world economy handed on as a legacy from the past.

The awareness that the high real long-term rate of interest is an ongoing problem has even spread to such venues as the G-7 summits and the International Monetary Fund. Yet the subjective and objective obstacles to effective action persist.

Irving Fisher concluded his masterpiece with words of caution about the predictive value of any interpretation of a phenomenon as complex as the interest rate: 'Were it possible to estimate the strength of the forces thus summarized, we might base upon them a prediction as to the rate of interest in the future. Such a prediction, however, to be of value, would require more painstaking study than has ever been given to this subject'.[2] Fisher himself was unable fully to follow this wise advice. In the last section of his book, he sketched, even if cautiously, a prediction of lower rates in the coming years, the early 1930s. The deflation that accompanied the crash of 1929 dramatically refuted his prediction: in the years that followed, real interest rates reached some of the highest levels in the history of capitalism.[3]

Keynes's approach is even more discouraging of the attempt to foresee the future path of the price of money. Unlike Fisher's, it does not seek to validate a theory by an empirical test of its

<hr>

[2] Fisher, *The Theory of Interest*, op. cit., 505–6.

[3] In *The Man Without Qualities*, Musil has peace celebrations staged on the eve of the war.

predictive capacity. Rather, it emphasizes the normative aspect, lest economic growth be stunted by an interest rate that is too high for the needs and opportunities of productive investment. It discourages attempts to specify a list of feasible and opportune measures, as a sort of 'prescription' for the world economy.

In this book we have not tried to show that Keynesian theory is always superior to the neo-classical view. We hope to have succeeded in calling forth Keynes's theory, too often forgotten, in the face of the contemporary problems of the world economy. Our reasons are both analytical and political. The Keynesian theory of interest, based on the possibilities opened up by an understanding of history, is better adapted than neo-classical theory, based on the unchanging repetition of a necessary calculation, to the environmental conditions of the past and our own present, with the disruptions and the difficulties of economic management reviewed above. Even if 'neo-classical' policies aimed at reducing the natural rate of interest by increasing the propensity to save were widely and successfully applied, a reduction in nominal rates would still require the international coordination of economic policies and the safe insertion of expansionary monetary policies in a coordinated framework, the very feasibility of which is the central concern of Keynesian theory. Were this not to occur, monetary policy could fail to transmit the impulse toward rate reduction from the short-term end to the long-term end of the maturity spectrum. It could even provoke the contrary effect, by raising long-term rates.

There is an asymmetry in the 'loss function' of economic policy-makers. The possible negative consequences of accepting the neo-classical theory of the natural rate of interest and not using economic policy are more serious, should neo-classical theory turn out to be wrong, than those of accepting Keynesian theory and using policy, should Keynesian theory turn out to be wrong. In the former case, if real long-term interest rates failed to fall, even without returning to the negative levels reached in the 1970s, the weight of their external debt would again burden the developing countries; the transformation of the economies of Eastern Europe would be even slower and less certain; industrial countries with a high public debt, like Italy, would be seriously hindered from putting their fiscal policies in order; and, investment, growth, and employment would be reduced throughout the world economy.

The reader may wonder what economic policy the authors have in mind to conclude this long argument showing that the high cost of money is a crucial, though also soluble, problem. No exhaustive answer can be given here, since our essay has not aimed to propose specific measures to reduce the cost of money. What we must provide, however, is a synthetic statement on the ultimate meaning of our reappraisal of Keynes's theory of interest.

This has nothing to do with the government activism normally associated with the Keynesian message, leading to the parable of 'digging holes', which is pernicious because it is so frequently misunderstood. The central point lies, rather, in the *capacity to govern*, which constitutes the premise of our argument. Any intervention by government must affirm this capacity and, in so doing, dictate the 'conventions' and make them worthy of trust. Fiscal policy and the budget, more than anything else, are the main vectors of a government's image. Fiscal policy, above all, must reflect the ability of the State to steer the economy. This must be expressed not in a mechanistic subservience to fixed rules, be they 'Keynesian' or 'neo-classical'. Rather, it must command assent by grasping the problems that the variety of history confronts us with and set them on the road to solution.

Today this capacity is limited. In what remains, despite everything, the world's premier economy, the United States, it has proved impossible for fiscal policy to arrest the decline in saving, the 'short-sighted preference for immediate consumption at the expense of investment.'[4] In Europe's leading economy,

---

[4] R. Kahn, 'Memorandum of Evidence Submitted to the Radcliffe Committee', in *Selected Essays on Employment and Growth* (Cambridge: Cambridge University Press, 1972), 126. For the complete proceedings of the Committee, see Radcliffe Committee, *Report of the Committee on the Working of the Monetary System* (London: HMSO, 1959); *Principal Memoranda of Evidence* (London: HMSO, 1960); *Minutes of Evidence* (London: HMSO, 1960). On Keynes's aversion to persistent budgetary deficits

Germany, taxpayers proved reluctant to shoulder the costs of reunification. In Japan, even though the course to be taken is clearly seen, with the economy on the verge of a 'debt-deflation', there are serious difficulties in reconciling opposing interests in an economic policy that is internally and internationally advantageous.

Nonetheless, a reduction in the cost of money can only come from a recovery in the capacity to govern. This should extend the scope for coordination among economic policies, even though these policies remain tied to the specific features of the different capitalisms.

A sort of 'money illusion' risks deflecting economic policy, leaving it content with a decline in nominal interest rates. A fall in real interest rates should not be entrusted to the brutality of recession and unemployment. Rates cannot be pushed down by a single country, with imprudent action by its central bank to force an expansion of the money supply, lacking the necessary support of rigorous fiscal and incomes policies. It is rather the rationality of conscious economic policies, coordinated in a global economic management, that must turn this largely conventional price toward non-inflationary growth. It depends on us, and also on our economic culture.

and his fear that they would boost liquidity preference and interest rates, see J. A. Kregel, 'Budget Deficits, Stabilisation Policy and Liquidity Preference: Keynes's Post-War Policy Proposals', in F. Vicarelli (ed.), *Keynes's Relevance Today* (London: Macmillan, 1985). This is the other important book on Keynes by Fausto Vicarelli, to whom our essay is dedicated with a remembrance and an esteem that the passing of time from his sudden death does not diminish.

THE MAIN TRENDS OF REAL INTEREST RATES (1960–1994)

An Essay by
A. Levy and F. Panetta

1

The Evolution of
Real Rates in the Leading
Industrial Countries

THE TRENDS

In analysing the essential features of the evolution of real inter-
est rates in the last three decades, reference will made to the
Group of Seven (hereafter G-7: United States, Japan, Germany,
France, Italy, United Kingdom and Canada).

The evolution of real interest rates over the past thirty years
can be divided into three phases. In the first—the 1960s and early
1970s—real rates were positive, modest (just over 2 per cent)
and stable. In the second phase—the 1970s—nominal yields
lagged behind inflation, producing negative real rates; this
coincided with an increased variability in inflation and in real
interest rates. Finally, in the first half of the 1980s, real yields
returned to positive values at levels unprecedented in the previous 150 years, while remaining variable (see Table 4 at the
end of this chapter); in the second half of the decade rates fell
slightly and stabilized somewhat (see Figs. 9 and 10).

Examining real yields in the individual countries, we can dis-
cern some specific features. At the beginning of the 1980s, the
United States reached especially high levels as compared with
previous periods and with other countries (Fig. 9 and Table 5).
The rate in Japan fell to its greatest negative values in the 1970s,
in concomitance with a period of high inflation by Japanese

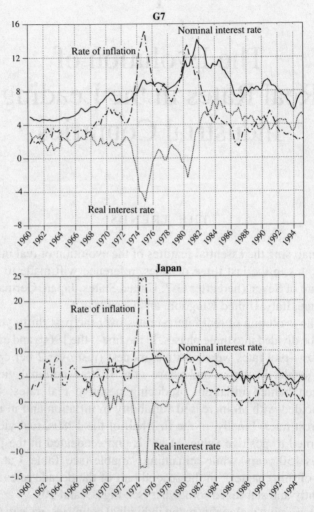

Fig. 9. Long-term nominal interest rate, rate of inflation, and long-term conventional real rate of interest in G-7 countries, the United States, Japan, and Germany, 1960–1995Q1

Sources: OECD, IMF.

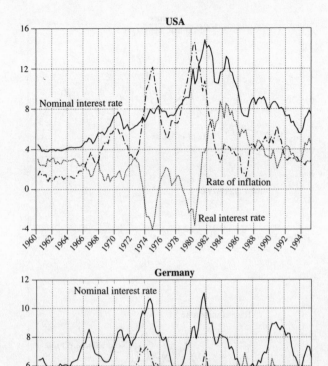

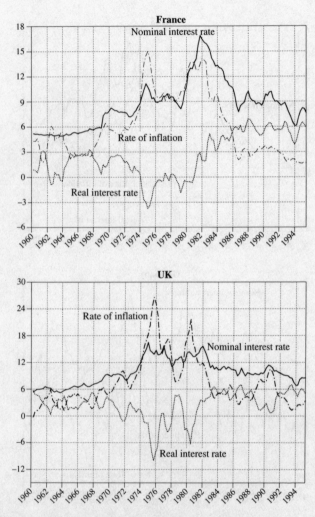

Fig. 10. Long-term nominal interest rate, rate of inflation, and long-term conventional real rate of interest in France, Italy, the UK, and Canada, 1960–1995Q1

Sources: OECD, IMF.

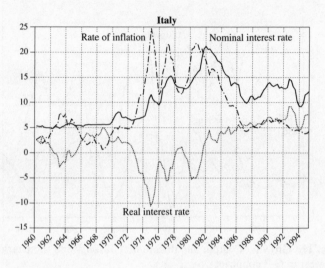

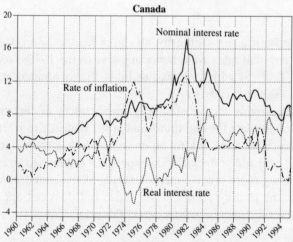

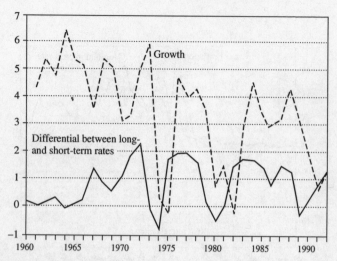

Fig. 11. Growth of output and differential of long- and short-term interest in G-7 countries

standards (Fig. 9). Going by all the indicators used, German long-term real rates were never negative in the 1970s (see Fig. 9 and Table 5) with a marked stability that continued into the 1980s (Tables 6 and 7).

These trends are substantially independent of the method used to calculate the real rates[1] and of the maturity to which the nominal rates refer. Taking an *ex ante* rate (based on some uncertain estimate of the inflation expected)[2] rather than an *ex post* rate (using more precise measurements of the actual inflation) affects the turning points in the series but does not appear to alter the fundamental tendencies[3] (Table 5).

---

[1] For a description of the different methods of calculating the indicators of real rates see Appendix 1.

[2] The estimate of an *ex ante* real rate for Italy and an examination of the methodological problems connected with this can be found in G. Carosio and I. Visco, 'Nota sulla costruzione di un tasso d'interesse reale', *Bollettino della Banca d'Italia* (1977), no. 4, 1–15.

[3] The index of correlation among the various pairs of real rates is, on average, 0.81; moreover, linear regressions of realized inflation on the ARIMA and OECD forecasts, not reported, show that the latter were more accurate.

Similar remarks apply to short-term and long-term nominal rates: in the period under study, the distinction does not affect the trends of the rates, nominal or real. However, over the last thirty years the slope of the yield curve has generally been positive, with long-term rates higher than short-term ones, save for a few brief interludes, but with wide oscillations (Fig. 11). Recent literature has highlighted the importance of this indicator as a predictor of economic activity.[4] for the United States. Fig. 11 seems to confirm the close correlation between the differential between long- and short-term rates and future growth of output for the G-7 countries. Although important, this aspect will not be dealt with in the present study.

VARIABILITY

Besides the trends in the level of interest rates, these decades were also distinguished by alternate stages of greater and lesser variability. For the seven countries as a whole, the periods of greatest turbulence were the first half of the 1970s and the first half of the 1980s (Tables 6 and 7). In the 1960s, characterized by lesser variability, US real rates were the most stable, Italian rates the most variable. In the 1970s and 1980s the greatest stability was found in the German rates; the greatest variability in the 1970s appeared in Japan and in Italy, in the 1980s in the United States and United Kingdom. From 1985 to 1990, the real rate in Italy was the most stable of all.

CONVERGENCE AND CORRELATION

The real interest rates prevailing in the various countries have gradually come to be more closely linked, reflecting the greater

[4] R. Laurent, 'An Interest Rate-based Indicator of Monetary Policy, Federal Reserve Bank of Chicago', *Economic Perspectives* (1988), no. 12, 3–14. For the United States, see, for example, A. Estrella and G. Hardouvellis, 'The Term Structure as a Predictor of Real Economic Activity', *Journal of Finance*, vol. XLVI (1991), 555–2276.

interdependence induced by international financial integration and, in Europe, by the tightening of exchange rate constraints.

A number of empirical studies have highlighted this point.[5] The strengthening of the link has taken various forms: a tendency of rates to converge, an increasing correlation between domestic and foreign rates, a growing importance of the role of world variables in accounting for domestic ones.[6]

In the present study, simple statistical tests of the significance of bilateral differentials between domestic rates seem to confirm the convergence of real rates in the last three decades, induced by financial integration and increased capital mobility. For each decade the following regression has been estimated:

$$R_{j,t} = a_0 + a_1 D_{j,t}^1 + \ldots + a_{n-1} D_{j,t}^{n-1} + e_{j,t}, \begin{cases} j = 1, 2, \ldots, n-1 \\ t = 1, 2, \ldots, T \\ n = 7 \end{cases}$$

where:

$R_{j,t}$ = long-term real interest rate of country j

$D_{j,t}^k$ = country dummy, equal to 1 when $k = j$ and 0 if $k \neq j$

$e_{j,t}$ = error term

In order to evaluate whether the mean real rate of the ith country is different from the mean rate of the jth country, the following hypothesis has been subjected to verification:

$$\mathbf{H}_0 : a_i = a_j, \qquad i \neq j, i \neq n, j \neq n.$$

[5] P. Atkinson and J. C. Chouraqui, 'The Origins of High Real Interest Rates', *OECD Economic Studies* (Paris, 1985), no. 5, 7–55; M. Fukao and M. Hanazaki, 'Internationalisation of Financial Markets and the Allocation of Capital', *OECD Economic Studies* (Paris, 1987), no. 8, 35–92; W. Tease *et al.*, 'Real Interest Rate Trends: the Influence of Saving, Investment and Other Factors', *OECD Economic Studies* (Paris, 1991), no. 17; R. J. Barro and X. Sala i Martin, 'World Interest Rates', NBER Working Paper (1990), no. 3317.

[6] From the estimates performed by R. J. Barro—'World Interest Rates and Investment', NBER Working Paper (1991), no. 3849—it emerges that the world variables account for the common component (or average) of the evolution of national real rates in these last years, but do not account for the persistent divergences among national rates: for example, according to the author's calculation, at the start of 1991 the short-term real rate in the United States was 0.2 per cent, the mean European rate 5.9 per cent.

To evaluate whether the mean real rate of the nth country is different from the mean rate of the ith country, the null hypothesis has been verified:

$$\mathbf{H}_0: a_i = 0.$$

Table 8 shows that the number of bilateral differentials that are non-significant at 5 per cent, marked with an asterisk, increased from 3 in the 1970s to 9 in the 1980s.[7] In the 1980s Japanese rates diverged significantly from the US and German rates; those of the EMS countries, i.e. Germany, France and Italy were very similar.

The evolution of the correlation between the domestic rates of the seven countries is also interesting. From the 1960s through the 1970s to the 1980s, the correlation between the mean real rate of G-7[8] and that of the individual countries gradually increased (Table 9). Using nominal rates, the trend is even more clear-cut (Table 10).

By country, in the 1960s the real rate of the United States showed the least correlation with the mean (Table 9), whereas in the 1970s and 1980s the most independent rate was that of Germany. Italy's rate was closely correlated with the mean in the 1970s, but not in the 1980s.

THE 'FISHER EFFECT'

Economic literature has devoted much attention to examining the so-called 'Fisher effect': that is, the hypothesis that the nominal interest rate is made up of a real rate, tending to be constant, and the rate of inflation anticipated by operators.[9]

---

[7] For the 1960s, the test excludes Japan, for which no series of long-term interest rates is available.

[8] In order to clear the correlation of the bias due to the different weights of the individual rates in the mean rate, the correlation is always calculated between the rate of a given country and the mean G-7 rate excluding that country.

[9] Among the many studies on the subject, see especially L. H. Summers, 'The Nonadjustment of Nominal Interest Rates: A Study of the Fisher Effect', in J. Tobin (ed.), *Macroeconomics: Prices and Quantities* (Oxford: Blackwell, 1983), 201–44;

However, empirical research on this theme has not reached any definite conclusions. On the basis of a few simple indicators proposed here no uniform tendency over time or between countries in line with Fisher's hypothesis can be found.

Apart from the graphic analysis, a first approximation of the presence of the Fisher effect is afforded by the correlation, country by country, between the nominal rate and its two hypothetical components. If the Fisher relation is verified, even approximately in our period, then most of the variations in the nominal rates should be caused by variations in the rate of inflation, not in real rates. The correlation between nominal and real rates should accordingly approach zero, that between nominal rates and expected inflation should approach one.[10]

Table 11 shows the indices of correlation between nominal and real rates and between nominal rates and inflation (actual and expected) for the three decades. For the seven countries as a group, the correlation of the nominal rate with actual inflation was much higher than that with the real rate in both the 1960s (0.76 against 0.14) and the 1980s (0.85 against –0.18), showing a relation not far distant from that proposed by Fisher. In the 1970s, however, the value of the two indices (0.8 and –0.63) signals the absence of this effect. Once again, Germany would seem to show a countertrend: a Fisher effect is evidenced in the 1970s (the indices are 0.81 against 0.11), but less clearly in the 1960s and 1980s.[11] Likewise, Figs. 9 and 10 suggest that the effect is present in the 1960s but less clearly so in the 1980s.

For the G-7 countries the correlations were also analysed for large cycles of inflation, taken as the periods between one trough and the next (see Figs. 9 and 10): 1967–72, 1972–8 and

F. S. Mishkin, 'The Real Interest Rate: a Multi-country Empirical Study', *Canadian Journal of Economics* (1984), no. 2, 283–311; and F. S. Mishkin, *Is the Fisher Effect for Real? A Reexamination of the Relationship between Inflation and Interest Rates* (NBER, Princeton: Graduate School of Business, Columbia University, Princeton University, 1991).

[10] This rule of thumb is a sufficient but not necessary condition; given its limitations, its results have a purely indicative value.

[11] Not dissimilar conclusions are obtained using expected rates of inflation calculated by various methods.

1978–86. In the first two cycles the difference between the absolute values of the two correlation indices is fairly small (0.92 and –0.63, 0.72 and –0.55, respectively). Fisher's hypothesis is slightly better confirmed in the 1978–86 cycle, where the correlations are 0.54 (between nominal rates and inflation) and –0.02 (between nominal and real rates).

The foregoing is confirmed by comparison of nominal interest rates and inflation rate trends in the ascending and descending phases of each cycle. In the first two cycles the difference between the curves in each phase is much greater than in the third cycle: in 1967–72 and 1972–8 inflation rose and fell more rapidly with respect to the nominal rate than it did in 1978–86, when movement in the two rates was more similar. In the last cycle this resulted in greater stability in the real interest rate.[12]

Nevertheless, even in 1978–86 the nominal interest rate did not rise and fall as fast as the rate of inflation: this caused the real rate to oscillate in a pattern reflecting changes in the inflation rate.

[12] In reading these findings it should be recalled that as the period of time considered diminishes, the probability of finding a Fisher effect increases.

Table 4. Long-term interest rates 1821–1990: weighted averages of United States, United Kingdom, Germany and France (decadal data)

	Nominal rate	Rate of inflation (consumer prices)	Real Rate
1821–30	4.6	n.a.	n.a.
1831–40	4.2	n.a.	n.a.
1841–50	4.3	–2.1	6.4
1851–60	4.0	1.8	2.2
1861–70	4.3	0.9	3.4
1871–80	3.9	–0.9	4.9
1881–90	3.2	–0.7	3.9
1891–1900	2.8	–0.5	3.3
1901–10	2.6	1.0	1.6
1911–20	3.5	10.1	–6.6
1921–30	4.7	2.3	2.4
1931–40	3.5	–0.8	4.3
1941–50	2.8	6.5	–3.6
1951–60	3.7	2.5	1.2
1961–70	5.1	2.7	2.4
1971–80	8.2	7.9	0.3
1981–90	10.4	5.3	5.1
1991–95 Q1	7.3	3.2	4.1

Source: see Appendix 3.

Table 5. Real interest rates[a]

	G-7	United States	Japan	Germany	France	Italy	United Kingdom	Canada
Conventional short-term rate								
1960–9	1.7	1.6	2.8	2.1	1.0	n.d.	1.9	1.9
1970–9	-0.8	-0.7	-1.5	1.8	-0.4	-2.0	-3.1	-0.3
1980–9	3.4	3.1	3.5	3.7	3.3	4.0	3.7	4.5
1990–4	2.8	1.0	2.8	4.3	6.1	5.9	3.8	4.8
Conventional long-term rate								
1960–9	2.3	2.3	n.d.	4.1	1.6	2.0	3.0	3.1
1970–9	0.1	0.4	-1.1	2.9	0.0	-1.9	-0.4	1.1
1980–9	4.3	4.8	4.1	4.5	4.1	3.2	3.6	4.9
1990–4	4.1	3.5	3.4	4.1	5.6	6.8	4.4	6.2
Short-term *ex post* rate								
1960–9	1.4	1.2	2.4	2.0	0.8	n.d.	1.4	1.7
1970–9	-1.4	-1.4	-1.5	1.6	-1.1	-3.8	-4.1	-0.9
1980–9	4.2	3.9	4.1	4.0	4.3	5.4	4.4	5.0
1990–4	3.6	1.6	3.8	4.7	7.1	6.8	5.9	5.8

Table 5. (*cont.*)

	G-7	United States	Japan	Germany	France	Italy	United Kingdom	Canada
Long-term *ex post* rate								
1960–9	1.9	1.9	n.d.	3.9	1.4	1.6	2.5	2.9
1970–9	-0.5	-0.3	-1.1	2.7	-0.7	-3.3	-1.5	0.4
1980–9	5.1	5.6	4.6	4.8	5.1	4.6	4.3	5.5
1990–4	4.7	4.0	4.0	4.1	6.1	7.5	5.9	6.9
Ex ante rate with OECD forecast								
1960–9	n.d.	n.d.	n.d.	n.d.	n.d.	n.d.	n.d.	n.d.
1970–9	-0.3	-0.1	-0.3	1.5	-0.5	-2.1	-2.4	0.2
1980–92	3.7	2.9	3.7	4.0	4.0	5.0	4.2	5.2
Ex ante rate with ARIMA forecast								
1960–9	n.d.	n.d.	n.d.	n.d.	n.d.	n.d.	n.d.	n.d.
1970–9	0.2	0.2	-0.2	2.5	1.6	-0.8	-1.8	0.2
1980–92	2.1	3.0	3.5	4.0	4.0	4.9	4.4	4.9

[a] For definitions see Appendix 1.
Sources: IMF and OECD data.

Table 6. Indicators of volatility: coefficient of variation of conventional real long-term rates[a]

	1960–4	1965–9	1970–4	1975–9	1980–4	1985–91
G-7	0.003	0.004	0.024	0.013	0.025	0.008
United States	0.003	0.006	0.022	0.015	0.034	0.013
Japan	—	—	0.051	0.024	0.014	0.007
Germany	0.009	0.007	0.010	0.007	0.009	0.008
France	0.013	0.008	0.019	0.010	0.018	0.006
Italy	0.017	0.014	0.046	0.031	0.030	0.006
United Kingdom	0.013	0.012	0.016	0.046	0.033	0.018
Canada	0.005	0.005	0.025	0.014	0.024	0.010

[a] Ratio between standard deviation and average; quarterly data.

Table 7. Indicators of volatility: coefficient of variation of long-term nominal rates[a]

	1960–4	1965–9	1970–4	1975–9	1980–4	1985–91
G-7	0.001	0.009	0.008	0.005	0.012	0.008
United States	0.002	0.008	0.006	0.008	0.013	0.010
Japan	—	—	0.009	0.011	0.010	0.011
Germany	0.002	0.006	0.010	0.010	0.011	0.011
France	0.001	0.008	0.011	0.006	0.016	0.008
Italy	0.009	0.002	0.011	0.010	0.026	0.011
United Kingdom	0.004	0.009	0.022	0.010	0.016	0.006
Canada	0.001	0.008	0.007	0.006	0.015	0.006

[a] Ratio between standard deviation and average; quarterly data.

Table 8. Significance of differentials between long-term real interest rates[a] (*t*-statistics).

	United States	Japan	Germany	France	Italy	United Kingdom	Canada
1960–72							
United States							
Japan	6.7						
Germany	-2.3	—					
France	2.3	—	9.1				
Italy	1.6*	—	4.4	-4.6			
United Kingdom		—	5.2	-3.9	0.7*		
Canada	3.9	—	2.8	-6.3	-1.6*	-2.4	
1973–80							
United States							
Japan	-1.5*						
Germany	4.8	-6.3*					
France	-0.4*	-1.1*	5.1				
Italy	-3.8	2.3	8.6	3.4			
United Kingdom	-1.5*	0.0*	6.3	1.1*	-2.3		
Canada	1.1*	-2.5	3.7	-1.4*	-4.9	-2.6	

Table 8. (*cont.*)

	United States	Japan	Germany	France	Italy	United Kingdom	Canada
1981–91							
United States							
Japan	−3.5						
Germany	−1.1*	−2.4					
France	−0.9*	−2.6	−0.2*				
Italy	−4.6	1.1*	3.5	1.7*			
United Kingdom	−3.5	0.0*	2.5	2.7	−1.0*		
Canada	0.0*	−3.5	−1.1*	−0.9*	−4.6	−3.6	

[a] The *t*-statistics refer to the following time-series cross-sectional regression:

$$R_{j,t} = a_0 + a_1 D^1_{j,t} + \ldots + a_{n-1} D^{n-1}_{j,t} + e_{j,t}, \qquad j = 1, 2, \ldots, n-1; \; t = 1, 2, \ldots, T; \; n = 7,$$

where:

$R_{j,t}$ = the long-term real rate of country j.

$D^k_{j,t}$ = dummy of country equal to 1 when k = j and equal to 0 if k ≠ 1,

$e_{j,t}$ = error term.

Table 9. Correlation between long-term conventional real rates (quarterly figures)

	G-7	United States	Japan	Germany	France	Italy	United Kingdom	Canada
1960–9								
G-7[a]	1	−0.445	—	0.242	0.224	−0.006	0.214	−0.379
United States		1	—	−0.434	−0.035	−0.568	−0.108	0.516
Japan			—			—	—	—
Germany				1	0.397	0.616	0.506	−0.409
France					1	0.532	0.029	−0.456
Italy						1	0.104	−0.519
United Kingdom							1	−0.148
Canada								1
1970–9								
G-7[a]	1	0.518	0.526	−0.010	0.702	0.748	0.236	0.600
United States		1	0.586	−0.092	0.768	0.658	0.284	0.670
Japan			1	−0.009	0.496	0.719	0.179	0.547
Germany				1	0.026	0.186	0.405	0.353
France					1	0.777	0.403	0.835
Italy						1	0.429	0.753
United Kingdom							1	0.410
Canada								1

Table 9. (*cont.*)

	G-7	United States	Japan	Germany	France	Italy	United Kingdom	Canada
1980–90								
G-7[a]		0.547	0.627	0.218	0.049	0.223	0.719	0.627
United States		1	0.820	0.420	0.504	0.699	0.883	0.666
Japan			1	0.442	0.444	0.613	0.759	0.454
Germany				1	0.726	0.624	0.559	0.626
France					1	0.865	0.660	0.613
Italy						1	0.737	0.624
United Kingdom							1	0.553
Canada								1

[a] The correlation between the G-7 average rate and the rate of each individual country is calculated by assigning to the country in question a weight equal to zero in the average rate.

Source: IMF.

Table 10. Correlation between long-term nominal rates (quarterly figures).

	G-7	United States	Japan	Germany	France	Italy	United Kingdom	Canada
1960–9								
G-7[a]	1	0.945	—	0.680	0.932	0.736	0.931	0.969
United States		1	—	0.415	0.919	0.464	0.919	0.981
Japan			—	—		—	—	—
Germany				1	0.278	0.373	0.385	0.308
France					1	0.352	0.924	0.922
Italy						1	0.402	0.406
United Kingdom							1	0.907
Canada								1
1970–9								
G-7[a]	1	0.638	0.464	0.024	0.860	0.530	0.416	0.948
United States		1	0.184	-0.222	0.591	0.729	0.603	0.942
Japan			1	0.617	0.638	0.109	0.671	0.330
Germany				1	0.145	-0.595	0.114	-0.197
France					1	0.608	0.826	0.715
Italy						1	0.648	0.803
United Kingdom							1	0.756
Canada								1

Table 10. (cont.)

	G-7	United States	Japan	Germany	France	Italy	United Kingdom	Canada
1980–90								
G-7[a]	1	0.895	0.862	0.859	0.962	0.927	0.867	0.969
United States		1	0.751	0.786	0.917	0.875	0.775	0.956
Japan			1	0.873	0.831	0.828	0.858	0.775
Germany				1	0.819	0.811	0.866	0.863
France					1	0.982	0.812	0.929
Italy						1	0.785	0.895
United Kingdom							1	0.852
Canada								1

[a] The correlation between the G-7 average rate and the rate of each individual country is calculated by assigning to the country in question a weight equal to zero in the average rate.

Source: IMF.

Table 11. Correlation between long-term nominal rate of interest, conventional real rate, and rate of inflation[a]

		1960–2	1963–5	1966–8	1969–71	1972–4	1975–7	1978–80
G-7	nom. rate –real rate	0.06	0.65	0.15	0.02	-0.97	-0.35	-0.77
	nom. rate –infl. rate	0.15	-0.18	0.26	0.84	0.98	0.53	0.94
United States	nom. rate –real rate	0.20	-0.14	-0.31	-0.03	-0.89	-0.25	-0.52
	nom. rate –infl. rate	0.41	0.65	0.73	0.80	0.92	0.42	0.85
Japan	nom. rate –real rate	—	—	—	-0.25	-0.95	-0.38	-0.13
	nom. rate –infl. rate	—	—	—	0.30	0.97	0.71	0.79
Germany	nom. rate –real rate	0.73	0.24	-0.22	-0.29	0.68	0.31	0.01
	nom. rate –infl. rate	-0.54	0.61	0.79	0.68	0.80	0.80	0.89
France	nom. rate –real rate	0.11	0.74	-0.57	0.43	-0.94	-0.22	0.47
	nom. rate –infl. rate	-0.06	-0.68	0.70	0.00	0.98	0.49	0.94
Italy	nom. rate –real rate	-0.44	0.76	0.47	-0.18	-0.74	0.08	-0.86
	nom. rate –infl. rate	0.67	-0.57	-0.42	0.86	0.87	0.33	0.93
United Kingdom	nom. rate –real rate	-0.50	-0.80	-0.33	0.37	-0.78	-0.02	-0.56
	nom. rate –infl. rate	0.65	0.90	0.60	-0.19	0.97	0.28	0.68
Canada	nom. rate –real rate	-0.34	-0.56	0.84	0.09	-0.72	0.11	0.88
	nom. rate –infl. rate	0.59	0.73	0.70	0.39	0.86	0.09	0.76

Table 11. (*cont.*)

		1981–3	1984–6	1987–91	1960–9	1970–9	1980–91
G-7	nom. rate –real rate	-0.59	0.72	-0.35	0.14	-0.63	-0.20
	nom. rate –infl. rate	0.86	0.95	0.78	0.76	0.80	0.84
United States	nom. rate –real rate	-0.51	0.93	0.17	-0.78	-0.52	0.11
	nom. rate –infl. rate	0.81	0.93	0.44	0.96	0.76	0.51
Japan	nom. rate –real rate	-0.56	0.10	0.17	—	-0.59	-0.13
	nom. rate –infl. rate	0.79	0.88	0.84	—	0.71	0.85
Germany	nom. rate –real rate	-0.08	-0.40	0.27	0.42	0.11	-0.48
	nom. rate –infl. rate	0.85	0.85	0.83	0.32	0.81	0.91
France	nom. rate –real rate	-0.30	-0.81	0.81	0.01	-0.75	-0.65
	nom. rate –infl. rate	0.79	0.98	0.11	0.46	0.89	0.95
Italy	nom. rate –real rate	0.29	-0.40	0.43	0.20	-0.25	-0.37
	nom. rate –infl. rate	0.47	0.98	0.63	0.15	0.67	0.83
United Kingdom	nom. rate –real rate	-0.75	-0.22	-0.52	-0.01	-0.45	-0.51
	nom. rate –infl. rate	0.94	0.61	0.72	0.62	0.75	0.78
Canada	nom. rate –real rate	-0.41	0.95	0.60	-0.40	-0.44	-0.35
	nom. rate –infl. rate	0.84	0.19	-0.05	0.85	0.70	0.78

[a] Consumer prices; quarterly data.

Source: IMF.

2

The Long-Term Relations Between Domestic and World Real Rates: *A Co-integration Analysis*

The foregoing discussion, especially the analysis of the relations in the evolution of real interest rates, suggests that in the 1980s ongoing international financial integration strengthened the link between domestic real rates and enhanced the role of external variables (for example, the mean real rate of the leading industrial nations) in accounting for the variables of individual countries.

In this section we shall seek to verify this proposition by empirically examining the link between domestic real rates and foreign real rates over three decades. The econometric exercise that follows represents a more detailed reworking, with more refined instruments, of the analysis of the convergence proposed in the previous section.

The theoretical scheme of reference is the Fisher equation,[1] on the basis of which in each period t is

$$\text{rea}_{t,j} = I_{t,j} - \Pi^e_{t,j} \tag{1}$$

that is, the expected real rate on a security with residual life $j(\text{rea}_{t,j})$ is equal to the difference between a nominal interest rate for the period in which the security is held, going from t to

---

[1] I. Fisher, *The Theory of Interest Rates* (London: Macmillan, 1930).

$t + j(I_{t,j})$, and the rate of inflation expected at period t to obtain between t and $t + j(\Pi^e_{t,j})$.

By transformations of (1) and on the basis of specific hypotheses of behaviour of the markets (rational expectations, uncovered interest parity and *ex ante* parity of purchasing power), described in detail in Appendix 2, we get a relation that can be empirically verified by econometric estimation, since it is composed of observable variables:

$$\text{rep}_{t,j} = \alpha + \beta \, \text{rep}^*_{t,j} + \eta_{t,j}, \tag{2}$$

where $\text{rep}_{t,j}$ is the *ex post* real rate that will obtain in the maturity period j, the asterisk indicates that the variable refers to the foreign country, and where $\eta_{t,j} = \beta \varepsilon^*_{t,j} - \varepsilon_{t,j} + u_{t,j}$ represents the error term.

Equation (8) enables the link between domestic and foreign real interest rates to be evaluated on the basis of the coefficient β. If $\beta = 0$, this link does not hold since one or more of the underlying hypotheses may be violated: rational expectations, uncovered interest parity, *ex ante* parity of purchasing power. If $\beta \neq 0$, there is a relation of equivalence or dependence between the domestic and the foreign rate, according to whether $\beta = 1$ or $\beta \neq 1$.

Estimating equation (8) with the ordinary least squares (OLS) method may, however, present problems, as is evinced by recent literature on co-integration:[2] if the real rates are not stationary variables, there may be difficulty in verifying the hypotheses (given that the asymptotic distribution of the estimators is not standard) and there is also the risk of spurious regressions (see Granger and Newbold)[3]. A further specific problem—evidenced by Cumby and Mishkin[4]—lies in the fact that the error term is

[2] For a review see, among the numerous studies on the subject, F. X. Diebold and M. Nerlove, 'Unit Roots in Economic Time Series: A Selective Survey', *Federal Reserve Board, Finance and Economics, Discussion Series* (1988), no. 49; and J. Y. Campbell and P. Perron, 'Pitfalls and Opportunities: What Macroeconomists Should Know About Unit Roots', *NBER Macroeconomics Annual*, 1991, 141–201.

[3] C. W. J. Granger and P. Newbold, 'Spurious Regressions in Econometrics', *Journal of Econometrics* (1984), no. 2, 111–20.

[4] R. E. Cumby and F. S. Mishkin, 'The International Linkage of Real Interest Rates: The European–U.S. Connection', *Journal of International Money and Finance* (1986), no. 5, 5–23.

not orthogonal to the variable $rep^*_{t,j}$, since the latter occurs at time $t+j$ and is thus correlated with the term of inflation forecasting error.

The co-integration approach enables these obstacles to be overcome,[5] if certain requirements hold (the two variables must be co-integrated), by providing consistent estimates of the co-efficients obtained with OLS, and also makes it possible to verify the existence of long-term relations without necessarily having to analyse the short-term dynamic of the variables as well.[6]

In examining the relations between domestic and foreign real rates, we shall stop at the so-called first stage of the analysis proposed by Engle and Granger:[7] the long-term static specification. Bivariate equations have been estimated in order to obviate the problem of a possible plurality of co-integration vectors.[8]

As a preliminary procedure, using the test for unit roots of Sargan–Bhargava (SB) and the Augmented Dickey–Fuller Test (ADF),[9] we shall verify the degree of integration of the individual series (domestic rates and mean G-7 rates, taking care to

[5] See, for example, G. Bodo, G. Parigi and G. Urga, 'Test di Integrazione e Analisi di Cointegrazione: una Rassegna della Letteratura', *Ricerche Economiche* (1990), no. 4, 389–436.

[6] This type of approach is, obviously, subject to some limitations, including the fact that the estimates obtained, although sizeable, are affected by a bias which seems to persist even in fairly numerous samples; the risk that, in increasing the size of the sample (e.g. in order to avoid the aforementioned problem of bias), structural changes in the relations considered may occur; and the limited power of the test owing to the presence of unit roots when the alternative hypothesis is represented by an autoregressive process whose coefficient is very close but not equal to one.

[7] R. F. Engle and C. W. J. Granger, 'Cointegration and Error Correction: Representation, Estimation and Testing', *Econometrica* (1985), no. 2, 251–76.

[8] See S. Johansen, 'Statistical Analysis of Cointegrating Vectors', *Journal of Economic Dynamics and Control* (1988), no. 12, 231–54.

[9] For the first of these see J. D. Sargan and A. Bhargava, 'Testing Residuals from Least Squares Regression for Being Generated by the Gaussian Random Walk', *Econometrica* (1983), no. 51, 153–74; for the second D. A. Dickey and W. A. Fuller, 'Likelihood Ratio Statistics for Autoregressive Time Series with a Unit Root', *Econometrica* (1981), no. 49, 1057–77, and S. E. Said and D. A. Dickey, 'Testing for Unit Roots in Autoregressive Moving Average Models of Unknown Order', *Biometrika* (1984), no. 71, 599–607. In order to rule out the possibility of the presence of a deterministic trend distorting the results of the tests, regardless of the properties of the series, in favour of the hypothesis of stationarity, three models have been estimated, with and without constant and trend, starting from the most general specification.

eliminate from this mean the individual country involved); if each of the two series is I(1), i.e. integrated by order 1, it will be possible to go on to estimate the static equations and verify the stationarity of their residuals—using the Co-integrating Regression Durbin Watson (CRDW) and ADF tests—in order to display a possible co-integration.

First, we shall examine the relations between the *ex post* real rate of each of the seven countries in turn and the mean rate of the other six. This will give some idea of the role played by the world real rate in determining domestic rates—a role whose importance has markedly increased over the last ten years, according to numerous studies.[10] Attention will then focus on some relations between pairs of domestic real rates.

Previous studies[11] have directly verified the stationarity in the differentials of the rates $(r - r^*)$. This procedure is equivalent to verifying the hypothesis, more restrictive than ours, that the co-integration parameter β is equal to 1, i.e. to verifying the equality among the real rates. Here, instead, we shall examine, by estimating the static equation, the long-term relation between variables, with an eye to the possibility that $\beta \neq 1$.[12]

In order to avoid performing estimates in periods where a structural break may have occurred, estimates and tests were run on the three main sub-periods that have characterized the evolution of real interest rates: 1960–72, 1973–80, 1981–91. This also made it possible to study how the relations have evolved in time.

[10] Barro and Sala i Martin, op. cit.

[11] See N. C. Mark, 'A Note on International Real Interest Differentials', *Review of Economics and Statistics* (1985), no. 67, 681–4; and A. M. Binotti, 'L'ipotesi di uguaglianza tra tassi d'interesse reali nei diversi paesi: una verifica empirica', *Ricerche economiche* (1990), no. 4, 443–54.

[12] As in recent empirical studies on convergence between macroeconomic variables (see H. S. Edison and E. O'N. Fisher, 'A Long Run View of the EMS', *Journal of International Money and Finance* (1991), no. 10; and P. G. Ardeni, 'On the Way to E.M.U: Testing Convergence of European Economies', *Economic Notes of the Monte dei Paschi di Siena* (1992), no. 2, 238–57) the reference here is to a stochastic definition of convergence on the basis of which if two series are cointegrated with parameter $\beta = 1$, then they are said to be convergent, since in the long term their levels tend to coincide; if instead $\beta \neq 1$, in the long term they do not converge but only have some common components.

As shown by Tables 16 and 17 in Appendix 3, the SB and ADF tests seem to indicate that in the 1960s all the domestic rates and the mean relative rates of G-7 were non-stationary and integrated by order 1.[13] However, on the basis of the CRDW and ADF statistics calculated on the residuals of the static equation, no pair of rates appears co-integrated—that is, there seems to be no long-term relation between domestic rates and mean foreign rate.

In the 1970s, the domestic rates and G-7 mean rates of almost all the countries appear stationary and hence the conditions for co-integration relations to exist are absent. Exceptions are the United Kingdom and Canada, whose series are not stationary, but for these cases it is not possible to rule out the null hypothesis of non-co-integration, i.e. the hypothesis that a long-term link is absent.

In the 1980s, lastly, almost all the domestic rates (though at different levels of significance) are integrated by order 1, but the G-7 mean rates appear stationary. This suggests that the non-stationary trends of the individual rates offset one another.

In order to remedy this drawback, the co-integration tests were applied to pairs of domestic rates (which the previous analysis had shown as integrated). Table 18 shows the static equations in which the Italian and French real rates are regressed in turn on the German rate; in a third equation the German rate is made to depend on that of the United States.[14]

In the 1980s, in contrast with the previous decades, for the pairs Italy–Germany and France–Germany the null hypothesis of non-co-integration (even if at a not particularly high level of significance) can be rejected and the relation has the sign expected. As expected, the Italian rate appears to be co-integrated with the German rate with a parameter (equal to 0.6) smaller than the French one (0.9); this last case seems to show a relation of near equality between the two rates. On the contrary, there

---

[13] The result is confirmed by the tests performed on the first differences, which were stationary.

[14] The existence of co-integration with the Japanese real rate was not verified, since in the 1970s and 1980s it was stationary, albeit weakly.

does not seem to be any relation of co-integration between the German and US rates in the three sub-periods.

To sum up, if co-integration analysis is employed, the hypothesis of a gradual increase over time in the interdependence between domestic and foreign real rates is supported by the data with reference to the European countries.

When the foreign real rate is approximated with the G-7 mean rate, in the 1960s and 1970s there does not seem to have been any significant relation with the domestic rates. Nor can one find a significant link between the two rates in the 1980s, but this may be attributable to the fact that the G-7 mean rate displays less variability in the individual rates of which it is made up.

If, to avoid this problem, we examine the relation between pairs of domestic real rates, a link, albeit a weak one, emerges in the 1980s between the French and Italian rates on the one hand and the German rate on the other, whereas no such co-movement appears between the US and the German rates.

With due caution, it can be concluded that in the 1960s and 1970s there was no close, long-term relation between domestic real rates and the world rate (of which the G-7 rate represents an approximation); in the 1980s, by contrast, one finds a link among the interest rates of the major countries of the European Monetary System.

3

Real Rates and Macroeconomic Variables

This chapter will analyse the trends of the principal theoretical determinants of real rates in the seven leading economies over the past thirty years. The evident abstraction represented by an analysis turning on the mean interest rate of the leading economies appears less heroic in the light of the empirical elements we have presented: the correlation between both nominal and real domestic and foreign rates tightened. Despite the fluctuations in exchange rates between the dollar, the yen and the basket of European currencies, international financial integration continued to cause the global variables to play an increasingly more important role than domestic variables in shaping the trends of real rates.

The theoretical link between real interest rates, saving and investment lies in the desired levels of these variables. The *ex post* identity between investment, saving, and current account deficits makes it difficult to identify the existence of an *ex ante* disequilibrium between capital demand and supply.

The evolution we describe authorizes us to identify long-term trends in saving rather than in investment as a possible determinant of the dynamics of real rates. The fall in real rates between the late 1960s and early 1970s followed the increase in the ratio of saving to income. Subsequently, the gradual decrease in this ratio contributed to the recovery of real rates by a greater amount than their initial fall. This development has frequently been interpreted as supporting neo-classical theories. Nonetheless, this interpretation loses some of its cogency when the trend of saving is analysed more carefully and when the distortions in accounts caused by the high inflation rates of the 1970s and early 1980s are taken into consideration.

We shall then describe the trends in other variables that may explain the phenomenon: namely, the return on capital and uncertainty in the financial markets, as measured by the volatility of prices for financial assets.

NATIONAL SAVING

According to classical economists, real interest rates are determined by real variables at a level that allows an equilibrium between saving and investment to be reached. Empirical analysis has revealed some of the essential factors in explaining the dynamics of saving.

In the industrial countries (OECD area) the average overall rate of saving (i.e. gross domestic saving as a proportion of gross product) shrank in the 1980s by more than 3 points compared with the mean of the two previous decades (21.3 per cent against 25.1 and 24.5 in the 1960s and 1970s respectively, Table 12).

Some leading industrial countries diverged from this overall trend. In the United Kingdom and Canada, if cyclical oscillations are ignored, the rate of saving decreased only moderately in comparison with the 1960s; in the United States and Japan it fell by around 3 points, whereas in Germany, France and Italy, where the phenomenon was more marked, it declined by between 5 and 6 points.

The rate of saving continued to grow through the 1960s and up to 1973, when it peaked at around 26 per cent. The two oil shocks were followed by two sharp falls, with the rate touching an absolute minimum (for the period of study) in 1983.

The second half of the 1980s (1986–9) saw a mild recovery in the rate in the area as a whole, especially in Germany and Japan (about 2 points).

Comparison of the saving levels in the various countries in

the 1980s shows that Japan recorded the highest rate in comparison with the OECD average (31.4 against 20 per cent), while the United States and United Kingdom had the lowest (between 16 and 17 per cent).

Saving in the public sectors

If the data for the private and public sectors are analysed separately, it can be seen that the latter was the chief architect of the trend in national saving, since private saving was relatively more stable over time.

Public saving decreased substantially in both the 1970s and 1980s compared with the average of the 1960s; the oil shocks of the mid-1970s and early 1980s led to sharp falls, which were strongly influenced by the cyclical trend.

The largest decreases in the period under examination occurred in Italy and Canada (by about 9 and 5 per cent respectively); the smallest was in Japan, where public saving as a proportion of output fell by 1.6 per cent; the United States, Germany and the United Kingdom occupy an intermediate position with a contraction of around 4 points.

In four countries (United States, Italy, United Kingdom and Canada) the decline in public saving exceeded that in national saving, though this was partly offset by a rise in private saving; in the other three (Japan, Germany and France), on the contrary, the fall was less than proportional and was accompanied by a fall in private saving.

As some empirical studies indicate, the actions of public and private operators do not appear to have offset one another, according to the so-called 'Ricardian equivalence'.[1]

Though public saving in the 1980s was lower than in the previous decades, it continued to increase in several countries. This positive outcome was an effect both of policies of fiscal

[1] See, for example, G. Nicoletti, 'A Cross-country Analysis of Private Consumption, Inflation and the Debt Neutrality Hypothesis', *OECD Economic Studies* (Paris, 1988), no. 11, 43–87.

Table 12. Rate of saving in the leading industrial countries (gross saving as percentage of gross output)

	1960–9	1970–9	1980–9	1990–4	1991	1992	1993	1994
United States								
national	19.7	19.4	16.3	15.2	15.5	14.4	14.7	16.0
public	2.0	0.4	-2.0	n.a.	n.a.	n.a.	n.a.	n.a.
private	17.7	19.1	18.3	n.a.	n.a.	n.a.	n.a.	n.a.
household	9.2	10.7	9.5	9.0	9.3	9.8	8.4	n.a.
corporate	8.5	8.3	8.9	8.9	9.1	8.4	9.2	n.a.
Japan								
national	34.5	35.3	31.7	33.5	35.1	34.0	32.5	31.2
public	6.2	4.8	4.9	n.a.	n.a.	n.a.	n.a.	n.a.
private	28.3	30.5	26.9	n.a.	n.a.	n.a.	n.a.	n.a.
household[a]	13.3	17.9	15.3	14.0	14.1	14.3	14.3	n.a.
corporate[a]	14.9	12.3	11.2	11.2	11.1	10.9	11.1	n.a.
Germany								
national	27.3	24.3	22.4	20.7	21.2	20.2	18.2	18.8
public	6.2	3.9	2.0	n.a.	n.a.	n.a.	n.a.	n.a.
private	21.1	20.5	20.3	n.a.	n.a.	n.a.	n.a.	n.a.
household[a]	6.9	8.7	7.9	n.a.	n.a.	n.a.	n.a.	n.a.
corporate[a]	14.2	11.8	12.8	12.4	12.3	11.5	10.7	n.a.
France								
national	26.2	25.8	20.4	19.9	21.0	19.9	18.1	19.0
public	n.d.	3.7	1.4	n.a.	n.a.	n.a.	n.a.	n.a.
private	n.d.	22.2	19.1	n.a.	n.a.	n.a.	n.a.	n.a.

household[a]	n.d.	13.6	10.3	9.2	9.0	9.5	9.7	9.3
corporate[a]	n.d.	8.5	8.5	10.8	10.4	10.8	10.8	11.5
Italy								
national	28.1	25.9	21.9	18.4	18.6	17.2	18.0	18.4
public	2.1	−5.1	−6.4	n.a.	n.a.	n.a.	n.a.	n.a.
private	26.0	31.1	28.4	n.a.	n.a.	n.a.	n.a.	n.a.
household	n.d.	24.5	21.1	19.2	20.1	20.0	18.3	17.5
corporate	n.d.	6.6	7.6	5.4	4.5	4.6	5.3	6.9
United Kingdom								
national	18.4	17.9	16.6	13.3	13.4	12.8	12.6	13.5
public	3.6	2.6	0.5	n.a.	n.a.	n.a.	n.a.	n.a.
private	14.8	15.3	16.1	n.a.	n.a.	n.a.	n.a.	n.a.
household	5.4	6.1	6.0	7.6	7.1	9.2	8.8	n.a.
corporate	9.4	9.2	10.1	7.0	5.9	6.8	8.6	n.a.
Canada								
national	21.9	22.9	20.7	14.5	14.1	13.0	13.6	15.8
public	3.6	2.7	−1.5	n.a.	n.a.	n.a.	n.a.	n.a.
private	18.3	20.1	22.2	n.a.	n.a.	n.a.	n.a.	n.a.
household	7.8	10.4	12.3	9.0	9.1	9.1	8.7	n.a.
corporate	10.5	9.7	9.9	7.7	7.7	7.2	8.2	n.a.
OECD[b]								
national	23.2	23.7	20.5	20.0	20.4	19.3	n.a.	n.a.

[a] Private saving may differ from the sum of its components owing to statistical discrepancies.
[b] Average 1990–2.

Source: OECD, National Accounts.

consolidation and of the long period of economic growth. In Japan the improvement was perceptible from the beginning of the decade; in Germany, France and the United Kingdom it started in the second half.

The United States and Italy registered anomalous trends: improvement was either nil or negligible and the public sectors continued to 'destroy' saving (in 1988 the negative balances were respectively 2 and 6 per cent).

Saving in the private sector

Overall, private saving was fairly stable over the three decades. Even individually, countries did not register wide variations in the period: the differences in saving rates between them are fairly small: at one end of the scale the United Kingdom recorded an average rate in the 1980s of 16.6 per cent, while Japan, at the other end, registered 26.6 per cent. The exceptions to this stability were the United Kingdom and Canada, where between the 1970s and 1980s the rate of saving rose by about 4 points, and Japan, where it fell by 3 points (Table 12). By contrast, in the 1980s, and especially in the second half, there was a fall in private saving in almost all the major countries, generally reflecting a decline in household saving.

The stability in private sector saving becomes all the more marked when compared with the variability in the rates of its components, i.e. households and firms. In line with the findings of empirical studies,[2] it appears that families are at least partly able to see through the corporate veil.

Household saving

If we leave aside the problem of inflation accounting (to which we shall refer below), there seems to have been an increase in

[2] See, for example, J. Poterba, 'Tax Policy and Corporate Saving', *Brookings Papers on Economic Activity* (1987), no. 2, 455–503.

household saving in the leading industrial countries during the 1970s, followed by a fall in the 1980s. This increase can be attributed to the high uncertainty prevailing in the 1970s, whereas the disinflation and higher growth rates in the 1980s had the opposite effect.

Corporate Saving

Corporate saving closely followed the pattern of profits. Following the fall of the 1970s, which was sharpest in Europe and Japan, the 1980s saw a reversal of trend: the weathering of the oil shock and the tight monetary policies, together with other factors, encouraged reorganization of the productive system; as a result of increased profitability, self-financing, and hence corporate saving, recovered.

Measuring national savings

Up to now we have adopted the traditional definition of saving, as used in national account. We have therefore ignored the methodological problems arising from the underestimation of income (and therefore of saving),[3] from the inclusion or exclusion of capital gains and losses,[4] and from the inclusion or exclusion of purchases of consumer durables in consumer expenditure.

A further problem in measuring savings is posed by the effects of inflation—in other words, the correction that aims to take account of the impact on interest earned of the rise in

[3] Two contrasting theses on the importance of errors in the measurement of income for evaluation of national saving are put forward by D. Blades, 'The Hidden Economy and the National Accounts', *OECD Occasional Studies* (Paris, 1982), and E. Feige, 'The Meaning of Underground Economy and the Full Compliance Deficit', in W. Gaertner and A. Wenig (eds.), *Studies in Contemporary Economics: Economics of the Shadow Economy* (Berlin: Springer Verlag, 1985), 100–20.

[4] See, for example, D. Bradford, 'Market Value vs. Financial Accounting Measures of National Savings', NBER Working Paper (1989), no. 2906.

inflation. For example, an increase in interest rates due to an expected rise in inflation will be reflected in an increase in saving, even though the wealth and purchasing power of the saver have remained unchanged. If the rates of inflation are expected to be positive, the inclusion of interest in income entails higher saving for net creditor sectors and decreased saving for debitor sectors.

The empirical analyses by Dean *et al.*[5] show that in the 1970s, when inflation was high, household saving may have been overestimated by several percentage points (as much as 7 and 5 for the United States and United Kingdom respectively); at the same time, national accounting data can be assumed to underestimate the public saving of the industrialized countries, especially those such as Italy where inflation and public debt are highest.

Thus if saving rates are adjusted for inflation, a somewhat different picture emerges, in which the variations are less pronounced or even reversed: for example, the period 1980–6 shows an appreciable rise in saving both in the United States (by 4 percentage points, as against a 3.5 per cent fall when the traditional measurement is used) and in Italy, where it would otherwise appear stable.

THE EVOLUTION OF GROSS INVESTMENT

With few exceptions, savings and investment in the majority of the OECD countries[6] substantially balanced one another in the 1960s and 1970s. In the 1980s the correlation between investment and savings within each country became appreciably weaker, mainly owing to increasing international capital mobility.

In the industrialized countries as a whole, the rate of investment (gross investment as a proportion of gross product) in the

[5] A. Dean, M. Durand, J. Fallon and P. Hoeller, 'Saving Trends and Behaviour in OECD Countries', *OECD Economic Studies* (Paris 1989), no. 14, 7–57.

[6] M. Feldstein and C. Horioka, 'Domestic Saving and International Capital Flows', *Economic Journal* (1980), 399–411.

1980s was a few points below that of the previous decades (20.9 per cent as compared with 22.9 and 23.4 in the 1960s and 1970s respectively). Despite the general recovery in the second half of the 1980s, the figures continued to lag behind those prevailing in the 1960s (Table 13).

The extent of the decline and the role of public and private components were not uniform.

In a first group of countries—Japan, Germany and France— there was a sharp fall of around 6–7 points, which can be largely ascribed to a dwindling of private investment. In the United States and United Kingdom, on the contrary, the decline was much more modest (1–2 points) and coincided with the contraction in public investment.

Despite this fall, Japan has maintained the highest investment rate (32.3 per cent in 1989, against an average of 21.5). In addition, the gap between the Japanese, German and French figures on the one hand, and those of the Anglo-Saxon countries on the other, was narrowed.

As already noted, the mid-1980s saw an appreciable revival in capital formation, both in relation to gross product and in terms of the rate of accumulation. Whereas the average annual growth of investment in the area had been 3.6 per cent in the 1970s and negative (–0.8) in 1980–3, in 1984–9 it rose to 5.8 per cent. In contrast, investment as a proportion of product rose by an average of 1 point in the area and about 3 points in the two countries, Japan and the United Kingdom, where the increase was largest.

The recovery of investment in the second half of the 1980s has been ascribed by Evans[7] and Ford-Poret[8] to a variety of factors, both real and financial:

• the favourable cyclical phase, with the long period of uninterrupted growth following the recession of 1981-82 generating strong capital demand;

[7] O. Evans, 'The Recent Behaviour of Business Fixed Investment in the U.S. and the Role of Computers', IMF Working Papers (1989), no. 97, 13–36.
[8] R. Ford and P. Poret, 'Business Investment: Recent Performance and some Implications for Policy', *OECD Economic Studies* (Paris, 1991), no. 16, 79–131.

Table 13. Investment in the leading industrial countries (gross investment as percentage of gross output)

	1960–9	1970–9	1980–9	1990–4	1991	1992	1993	1994
United States								
national	18.9	19.2	17.9	16.1	15.4	15.4	15.9	17.0
public	2.7	2.0	1.6	1.7	1.8	1.7	1.7	n.a.
private	16.2	17.2	16.3	14.2	13.7	13.7	14.3	n.a.
Japan								
national	34.7	34.5	29.6	30.6	31.8	30.7	29.8	28.6
public	4.4	5.4	5.3	5.6	5.1	5.7	6.6	n.a.
private	30.3	29.0	24.3	25.5	26.7	25.0	23.2	n.a.
Germany								
national	26.5	23.4	20.6	18.7	19.8	18.9	17.1	16.6
public	3.9	3.7	2.5	2.0	2.0	2.0	1.9	n.a.
private	22.6	19.8	18.0	17.1	17.7	16.9	15.1	n.a.
France								
national	25.2	25.4	20.8	19.9	21.2	20.0	18.6	18.1
public	n.d.	3.4	3.2	3.4	3.4	3.5	3.4	3.4
private	n.d.	22.0	17.6	16.5	17.8	16.5	15.2	14.7

Italy								
national	26.4	25.8	22.8	18.5	19.7	19.1	16.9	16.4
public	3.1	3.1	3.6	2.9	3.3	3.0	2.7	2.3
private	23.3	22.7	19.2	15.6	16.5	16.1	14.2	14.1
United Kingdom								
national	18.9	19.8	17.4	16.4	17.0	15.7	15.0	15.0
public	4.1	4.1	1.8	2.1	2.1	2.1	1.8	n.a.
private	14.8	15.7	15.6	14.7	14.9	13.6	13.2	n.a.
Canada								
national	24.2	24.5	22.2	19.2	19.5	18.7	18.1	18.6
public	4.2	3.4	2.6	2.4	2.4	2.3	2.3	n.a.
private	20.0	21.0	19.6	17.0	17.1	16.3	15.8	n.a.
OECD								
national	22.8	23.5	21.0	20.9	20.9	20.8	20.7	21.0

Source: OECD, National Accounts.

- the improvement in the profitability and balance-sheet situation of companies, which benefited from high cash flows, reduced indebtedness and the lower cost of raising of risk capital induced by high share prices, all of which led to an increased return on capital;
- less uncertainty in the markets than in the 1970s; the oil countershock in 1986 may have boosted confidence among operators;
- considerable technological progress, especially in computers; by lowering the cost and increasing the diffusion of capital, these innovations increased its productivity.

It is interesting to note how the growth in investments coincided with relatively high real interest rates compared with those of the previous decades; this would suggest that in the 1980s the influence exerted by investment on real rates was relatively stronger than the effect of real rates on investment.

RATES OF PROFIT IN INDUSTRY

One of the hypotheses put forward to account for the evolution of real rates is that they have reflected the trend in capital profitability.[9]

Neo-classical theory holds that the relationship between the rate of profit on productive capital and the real interest rate on financial capital is based on investment; the latter is increased by high rates of expected return on capital. The resulting pressure on available resources causes real interest rates to rise.

Here again the empirical analysis is based on an approximation, since the available data refer to the current return on

---

[9] See Atkinson and Chouraqui, op. cit., Dean *et al.*, op. cit., and G. Galli and F. Giavazzi (ed.), 'Tassi d'interesse reali e debito pubblico negli anni Ottanta: interpretazioni, prospettive, implicazioni per la politica di bilancio', *Il disavanzo pubblico in Italia: natura strutturale e politiche di rientro*, Ente 'L. Einaudi' (Bologna: Il Mulino, 1992), 277–356.

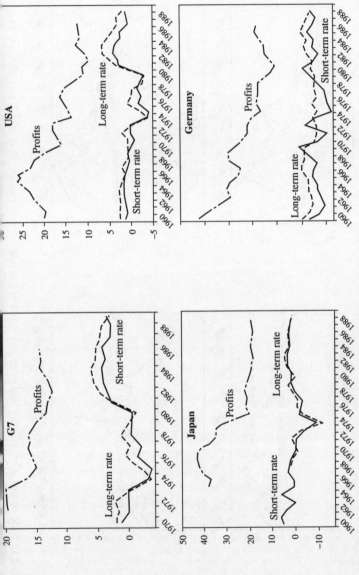

Fig. 12. Rate of profit in industry and conventional real interest rates in G-7 countries, the USA, Japan, and Germany

Sources: National accounts, OECD.

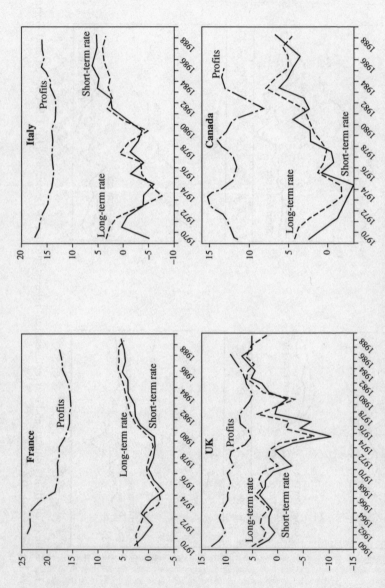

Fig. 13. Rate of profit in industry and conventional real interest rates in France, Italy, the UK, and Canada

Table 14. Capital productivity in industry[a]

	1960–9	1970–9	1980–9
G-7	—	17.3	13.8
United States	23.0	16.7	12.7
Japan	39.9	28.3	19.9
Germany	20.9	15.6	13.4
France	—	20.4	16.4
Italy	—	15.8	15.7
UK	10.3	7.3	6.7
Canada	15.8	13.1	12.1

[a] Capital productivity is defined as the ratio of gross operating margin and gross capital stock in the manufacturing industry; for Italy, the profits of the non-farm/energy sector and the capital stock of the private sector have been used.

Note: Annual data; sample: 1960–88 (for Japan 1965–88, France and Italy 1970–88).

Sources: OECD, op. cit; for Italy: Quarterly econometric model of the Bank of Italy.

existing capital, whereas the conceptually important variable is the expected return on new investment.

Rates of profit in industry have followed a very similar path in the major industrial countries.[10] In the 1970s nearly all the countries recorded a decline in capital profitability compared with the high levels of the 1960s (the early 1970s in Italy and France, as figures for the 1960s are not available). This can be seen from Figs. 12 and 13 and Table 14.

This trend was reversed at the start of the 1980s. Recovery from the oil shock, firmness of monetary policies and other factors encouraged the reorganization of productive systems. This was reflected in a general rise in rates of profit, starting in 1981–2. The rise was most evident in Germany and the

[10] These are calculated by the OECD, with a procedure homogeneous among countries, as the ratio between gross operating margin and gross capital stock in the manufacturing industry; for Italy a different indicator has been used, taken from the database of the quarterly econometric model of the Bank of Italy (profits in the non-farm/energy sector and capital stock of the private sector), which is thus not comparable with the other countries.

United Kingdom (between 4 and 5 per cent), somewhat less in the United States and Italy (about 3 per cent), and almost nil in Japan.

The link between rates of profit and real interest rates appears very weak if we consider the three decades as a whole. In the 1980s interest rates rose to much higher levels than those prevailing in the 1970s, while the opposite was true for rates of profit. The rise in the two variables observed in the 1980s is obviously not sufficient to re-establish a structural relation.[11]

The precarious nature of such a relation appears to be confirmed by linear regressions for 1960–90. Long-term real rates in the individual countries and the G-7 average have been regressed against rates of profit: the coefficients are generally of the wrong sign and not significant. Interesting exceptions are Italy and the United Kingdom, where there seems to be a relation that is both significant and has the expected sign; this link also emerges in the graphic evidence, especially for the United Kingdom (Fig. 13).

THE VOLATILITY OF THE FINANCIAL MARKETS

Under Fisher's theory, the nominal interest rate is composed of the real return on capital and an element intended to cover against price rises. The size of the second component depends on the amount of risk associated with the future evolution of the prices of the financial variables.

Assuming that takers of funds and savers are both averse to risk, an increase in uncertainty has a twofold effect: savers will require a greater return on their assets, while share issuers will demand a reduction in the cost of their liabilities. If both parties were equally averse to risk, the net effect on the real market rate would be nil, and the increased uncertainty would only cause activity on the capital market to diminish.

[11] This is the conclusion reached by Galli and Giavazzi, op. cit.

However, certain empirically confirmed considerations suggest that a positive premium for uncertainty is more likely. Firstly, in several countries issuers of securities are protected by clauses providing for advance refund: in this way the risks arising from adverse movements in the financial variables (e.g. a sharp drop in nominal rates) are limited, usually at low cost. Secondly, in all countries the state plays a very important role in the capital markets as a net taker of funds; since capital demand by the state is not affected by the increased uncertainty, at least in the short term, a rise in uncertainty will lead to a greater divergence between nominal rates and the rate of inflation.

In the neo-classical context the uncertainty to which economic agents refer is that associated with real rates. Examining the trend of G-7 rates, we can see that the coefficient of variation of real returns is higher in the first half of the 1980s (equal to 0.025; Table 6), accompanying the sharp fall in real and nominal rates; but the coefficient of variation was also high in 1970–4, although real returns were at record lows.

If a Keynesian-type model is used, the rise in real returns could be linked with the increase in nominal rates, due to the latter's volatility. However, no clear-cut relation emerges between the trend of real rates and the volatility of nominal returns, which evolve in a manner similar to real returns over the three decades (Table 7).

Similar conclusions emerge if we analyse a number of proxies for the volatility of the financial markets extracted on the basis of the trend of share prices (Table 15). In the 1980s market volatility was generally high; however, the maximum volatility in the stock markets occurred in the second half of the decade, when the upward surge in real rates was halted and then reversed. In addition, all the indicators employed show greater volatility in the period 1970–80 compared with the previous decade, when the real rates were positive, albeit low in absolute terms.

Table 15. Indicators of volatility of share indices

	1961–5	1966–70	1971–5	1976–80	1981–5	1986–90
Kurtosis of returns on shares						
United States	8.1	4.2	3.0	3.6	4.1	6.6
UK	3.7	4.0	8.6	3.4	2.7	9.9
France	3.3	2.6	13.4	3.2	7.2	5.5
Japan	10.9	8.2	2.2	2.6	3.2	3.4
Germany	5.9	3.9	2.2	2.8	2.6	8.5
Canada	3.9	3.4	4.2	6.2	3.6	12.7
Italy	2.5	4.4	3.0	2.9	4.6	4.2
AVERAGE	5.5	4.4	5.2	3.5	4.0	7.3
Percentage of months in which the absolute variation of the stock exchange index exceeded 5%						
United States	5.1	13.6	18.6	8.5	16.9	15.5
UK	6.8	13.6	44.1	32.2	18.6	31.6
France	25.4	20.3	35.6	40.7	35.6	34.5
Japan	32.2	6.8	37.3	1.7	11.9	35.1
Germany	20.3	11.9	18.6	6.8	18.6	26.3
Canada	8.5	15.3	23.7	32.2	28.8	25.0
Italy	33.9	13.6	35.6	47.5	44.0	41.0
AVERAGE	18.9	13.6	30.5	24.2	24.9	29.8

Range of variation[a]

United States	6.8	8.5	9.8	7.4	8.0	8.7
UK	7.2	8.9	16.7	12.8	8.1	12.0
France	11.2	9.7	18.0	14.6	18.7	12.7
Japan	15.5	7.7	8.9	4.3	6.6	11.8
Germany	11.4	8.1	10.0	6.0	6.3	11.9
Canada	7.1	9.6	12.7	12.9	11.8	11.6
Italy	12.6	9.4	14.1	16.1	14.8	17.7
AVERAGE	10.3	8.8	12.9	10.6	10.6	12.3

[a] Mean value of the difference between maximum and minimum variation of the share index.

Source: IMF data.

SOME REMARKS ON THE
POLICY MIX AND FINANCIAL AND
EXCHANGE DEREGULATION

Several studies have attributed the structural 'break' in the behaviour of real interest rates over the last decade to the sudden change in stance and operational framework of monetary policies in the early 1980s;[12,13] they also cite the strongly expansionary budgetary policies at the start of the decade (especially in North America) and the general failure to make active and flexible use of such policies, thus generating an unfavourable policy mix and a permanent 'overburdening' of monetary policies.

This approach has been criticized as being better-suited to describing the phenomenon in the short rather than long term, since it helps to account for the sharp variation in rates at the start of the decade, but not the persistence of the rates.

In view of the need to identify more structural, longer-term factors, a third line of analysis focuses on the profound and radical changes which financial systems have undergone in the last decade, with reference to deregulation and innovation and the greater efficiency this has generated.

The effects of these processes on real interest rates have not been uniform (for instance, some studies see the increased competition in lending among intermediaries as pushing down interest rates). On the whole, however, the changes seem to have had the net effect of raising rates.

In the 1960s and 1970s, nominal interest rates in several countries were subject to regulation, making variation difficult (for example, Regulation Q in the United States); this produced an inverse correlation between the rate of inflation and real interest rates. The arrival of market deregulation and the adoption of anti-inflationary policies by monetary authorities meant that in the 1980s nominal rates reflected expected and actual

[12] O. J. Blanchard and L. H. Summers, 'Perspectives on High World Real Interest Rates', *Brookings Papers on Economic Activity* (1984), no. 2, 273–324.

[13] Dean *et al.*, op. cit.

inflation more rapidly and more closely, which led to higher and more stable real rates.

This is suggested by the experience of Germany, where interest rates have never been subject to administrative controls: nominal interest rates have followed the trend of inflation more faithfully than in any other country throughout the entire period under study.

A further important factor appears to have been exchange deregulation and the resulting increase in international capital mobility in the last decade. This may have brought about a levelling of interest rates compared with sometimes higher rates in the leading countries: US rates at the start of the 1980s and German rates most recently.

This line of analysis is also especially effective in accounting for the evolution and high levels of interest rates in the EMS countries, where increased constraints on exchange rates have strengthened the guiding role played by the German interest rates.

4

Summary of the Empirical Evidence

The most striking feature to emerge from the analysis of the trend of real rates over the past thirty years is the high mean level of rates in the 1980s as compared with the previous decades, plus the fact that nominal rates have not diminished even in periods of low inflation such as the mid-1980s.

Furthermore, the link between the real rates in the G-7 countries—and hence the interdependence of the system—has gradually become tighter, as a result of international financial integration and, in Europe, stronger exchange rate constraints. The empirical evidence shows a growing convergence and correlation between domestic and foreign rates, albeit to a varying degree, and bears witness to the ever-increasing importance of international variables in accounting for domestic ones.

By contrast, the data do not appear to support the existence of the so-called 'Fisher effect'—the hypothesis that the nominal interest rate is composed of the real rate, which tends to be constant over time, and the rate of expected inflation.

In addition, previous analysis of convergence has been pursued in greater depth. This entailed using co-integration analysis to verify the proposition that the link between domestic real rates has been strengthened by international financial integration. Notwithstanding the intrinsic limitations of these methodologies, the results of the tests appear to support the hypothesis: whereas in the 1960s and 1970s there seems to have been no significant relation between real rates and the world rate (approximated as the mean rate of the G-7 countries), a link between the real rates of the leading countries in the European Monetary System emerges in the 1980s.

Keynes's theory of interest is not immediately verifiable by econometric means. The task would be to find the correspondence of a historical series with various models constructed on the basis of market conventions in the different periods, and not just with a single model for the entire period.

Neo-classical theory has instead indicated a series of factors that may have affected the phenomenon. Some of these, such as the change in policy mix, help to account for the evolution of real rates in specific periods. But, taken as a whole, the trend of the variables examined does not provide a coherent explanation for the entire thirty-year period.

Again, the most common interpretation used in the past, which is based on the interaction between a declining savings trend and the sustained pattern of investment, supplies only a partial, and in some respects only apparent, explanation. In the 1980s the overall rate of saving of the industrial countries was lower than in the previous decades; this holds true both for the private component (according to recent studies, this was affected by the fall in world income after the second oil shock, which was judged to be temporary and hence compensated by a reduction in savings) and the public component (especially as regards the United States). At the same time, high rates of capital accumulation were recorded, thus generating a large demand for funds, with both being stimulated by the high return on capital. An indication of the latter may be the general strengthening over the decade of the relation between the operating margins and capital stock of firms and the high prices of securities. Nevertheless, investments as a proportion of output and indicators of expected capital return were both lower in the 1980s than in the 1960s, when real rates were appreciably lower. Moreover, the very dynamic of saving and investment was affected by the distortions induced by high inflation rates.

A not inconsiderable influence on interest rates may have been exerted by uncertainty over the future course of inflation and the returns on financial assets. The underlying idea is that savers require a larger return where the stocks held carry greater risk. This thesis does not appear to be validated by measurements of the volatility of real and nominal returns: the maximum volatility of the stock markets in the countries studied was actually recorded in the second half of the 1980s, when the upswing in real rates was first halted and then reversed.

Lastly, brief mention has been made of two other approaches that attempt to account for the structural 'break' in the behaviour of real rates over the last decade. The first makes reference to the sudden change in stance and operational framework of US monetary policy at the outset of the 1980s, to which were added strongly expansionary budget policies (especially in North America) and the general failure to make active, flexible use of these policies, thus producing an unfavourable policy mix and a permanent 'overburdening' of the monetary policies. The other line of analysis concentrates on the profound and radical changes undergone by financial systems in the last decade, with reference to deregulation and innovation and to the resulting increase in efficiency.

APPENDIX 1

Various Indicators of Real Rates

In analysing real rates of interest a preliminary problem arises from the impossibility of observing the expected rate of inflation. Therefore, in order to evaluate the robustness of the analyses performed and the results obtained, various indicators of real rates have been used.

The data given in the graphs and tables are on a quarterly basis. Let p_t be the index of consumer prices in the quarter t, and i_t and r_t the nominal and real interest rates; the inflation rate, π_t, is calculated as

$$\pi_t = (\ln p_t - \ln p_{t-4}) \cdot 100,$$

or as the percentage variation of the consumer price index with respect to the corresponding period of the previous year.

The nominal short- and long-term rates employed are described in Appendix 3. The indicators used for the real rates are described in what follows.

Real 'conventional' rate: nominal rate in the period t deflated with the inflation rate in the 12 months ending at t, or

$$r_t = (1 + i_t) / (1 + \pi_t).$$

Real *ex post* rate: nominal rate in the period t, deflated with year on year inflation that occurred in the 12 months following t, or

$$r_t = (1 + i_t) / (1 + \pi_{t+4}).$$

The use of this indicator is tantamount to a hypothesis of rational expectations with perfect forecasting ability.

Real *ex ante* rate with OECD forecast: nominal short-term rate in period t deflated with the rate of increase of the GDP deflator forecast by OECD; since 1972 these forecasts have been made twice a year (for the 12 following months) and published in *Economic Outlook*.

Real *ex ante* rate with ARIMA forecasts: nominal short-term rate at period t deflated with an ARIMA forecast of the inflation rate in period t. This forecast is obtained with an ARIMA-type equation $(1,1,1)$ of the price index:

$$d \ln p_t = \alpha d \ln p_{t-1} + \beta \varepsilon_{t-1}.$$

The expected inflation for period t is obtained from the recursive estimate (i.e. stopping the sample at $t - 1$) of this equation with a dynamic simulation of a period outside the sample; this method corresponds to assuming that the agents know the structure of the model that generates inflation.

APPENDIX 2

From the Fisher Equation to the Relation of Co-integration Subjected to Estimate

The starting relation is the Fisher equation,[1] according to which in each period t is

$$\text{rea}_{t,j} = I_{t,j} - \Pi_{t,j}^e; \tag{1}$$

that is, the expected real rate on a security with residual life $j(\text{rea}_{t,j})$ is equal to the difference between a nominal interest rate for the period in which the security is held going from t to $t+j(I_{t,j})$ and the expectation at period t of the inflation rate that will prevail between t and $t+j(\Pi_{t,j}^e)$.

Under the hypothesis of rational expectations and defining the forecasting error $\varepsilon_{t,j}$ as

$$\varepsilon_{t,j} = \Pi_{t,j} - E(\Pi_{t,j} \mid \Omega_t),$$

where the term $E(\Pi_{t,j} \mid \Omega_t)$ indicates the expected value of $\Pi_{t,j}$ conditional on the information available to the agents at time $t(\Omega_t)$, we can say that

$$E(e_{t,j} \mid \Omega_t) = 0. \tag{2}$$

On the basis of this assumption, (1) can be rewritten as

$$E(\text{rep}_{t,j} \mid \Omega_t) = I_{t,j} - E(\Pi_{t,j} \mid \Omega_t),$$

where $\text{rep}_{t,j}$ is the *ex post* real rate that will obtain in the maturity period j.

Two relations relevant to our purpose are the uncovered parity of the interest rates,

$$I_{t,j} - I_{t,j}^* = E[(s_{t,j} - s_t) \mid \Omega_t], \tag{3}$$

---

[1] Fisher, op. cit.

and the parity of purchasing power in the *ex ante* version,

$$E[(\Pi_{t,j} - \Pi_{t,j}^*) \mid \Omega_t] = E[(s_{t,j} - s_t) \mid \Omega_t], \tag{4}$$

where s_t is the logarithm of the spot exchange rate at time t and the asterisked variables refer to the foreign country.

Combining equations (3) and (4) we obtain the condition of equivalence between the *ex ante* real rates of two countries:

$$
\begin{aligned}
[I_{t,j} - E(\Pi_{t,j} \mid \Omega_t)] &- [I_{t,j}^* - E(\Pi_{t,j}^* \mid \Omega_t)] \\
&= E[(\mathrm{rep}_{t,j} - \mathrm{rep}_{t,j}^*) \mid \Omega_t] \\
&= \mathrm{rea}_{t,j} - \mathrm{rea}_{t,j}^* \\
&= 0.
\end{aligned}
\tag{5}
$$

Equation (5) can be empirically verified by econometric estimate of the equation

$$\mathrm{rea}_{t,j} = \alpha + \beta\, \mathrm{rea}_{t,j}^* + u_{t,j}. \tag{6}$$

By using the relation

$$\mathrm{rep}_{t,j} + \varepsilon_{t,j} = \mathrm{rea}_{t,j}, \tag{7}$$

equation (6) can be rewritten in terms of observable variables as follows:

$$\mathrm{rep}_{t,j} = \alpha + \beta\, \mathrm{rep}_{t,j}^* + \eta_{t,j}, \tag{8}$$

where

$$\eta_{t,j} = \beta \varepsilon_{t,j}^* - \varepsilon_{t,j} + u_{t,j}.$$

Equation (8) enables the link between domestic and foreign real rates of interest to be evaluated by looking at the coefficient β: if $\beta = 0$ this link is not verified, since one or more of the underlying hypotheses is violated: rational expectations, uncovered interest rate parity and *ex ante* parity of purchasing power. If $\beta \neq 0$ there is a relation of dependence or equivalence between the domestic and the foreign rate, according to whether $\beta \neq 1$ or $\beta = 1$.

APPENDIX 3

Data Utilized and Sources

THE 1960–1994 SERIES

The consumer price indices and interest rates utilized have been taken from the *International Financial Statistics* tapes of the IMF, except for the long-term rates of Italy, which come from the Bank of Italy.

The average rates of the leading seven countries are weighted with their gross domestic product converted at purchasing power parity; source: OECD, *National Accounts*.

For each country the short- and long-term interest rates are derived, respectively, from the returns (gross, unless otherwise stated) on the following instruments:

United States: three-month Treasury bills; 10-year state bonds.

Japan: Call money rate; 7-year state bonds.

Germany: 3-month interbank deposits; basket of public sector bonds with residual life of more than three years.

France: day-to-day interbank deposits; basket of public sector bonds with residual life of more than five years.

Italy: inter bank call rate; average net return on Treasury bonds with residual life of more than one year quoted on the Milan Stock Exchange.

United Kingdom: 3-month Treasury bills; 20-year state bonds.

Canada: 3-month Treasury bills; state bonds with residual life of more than ten years.

THE 1840–1959 SERIES

The long-term interest rates are taken from S. Homer and R. Sylla:[1]

United States: long-term state bonds.

United Kingdom: 3 per cent Consols.

Germany: long-term bonds, Prussian till 1883, Imperial German from 1884 to 1908; from 1909 to 1959 High grade bonds.

France: long-term state bonds.

The US consumer price indices are taken from *U.S. Historical Statistics*;[2] those of Germany and France from Mitchell;[3] those of the United Kingdom from Rousseaux[4] and Mitchell.[5]

The annual series of GNP converted at purchasing power parity, used for weighting the average rate of the four countries, are taken from Maddison.[6]

[1] S. Homer and R. Sylla, *A History of Interest Rates* (New Brunswick: Rutgers University Press, 1991).

[2] US Department of Commerce, *U.S. Historical Statistics* (Washington, 1985).

[3] B. R. Mitchell, *European Historical Statistics 1750–1970* (London: Macmillan, 1975).

[4] P. Rousseaux, *Les Mouvements de Fonds de l'Economie Anglaise 1800–1913* (Brussels: L'Edition Universelle, 1938).

[5] Mitchell, op. cit.

[6] A. Maddison, *Phases of Capitalist Development* (New York: Oxford University Press, 1982).

Table 16. Unit root test on long-term real rates (quarterly figures)

		Sargan–Bhargava Test	
		H_0: random walk (1)	H_0: random walk with drift (2)
1960–72			
United States	real rate	0.42	0.45
	G-7 average rate	0.29	0.19
Germany	real rate	0.35	0.23
	G-7 average rate	0.65	0.66
France	real rate	0.37	0.35
	G-7 average rate	0.67	0.66
Italy	real rate	0.18	0.11
	G-7 average rate	0.67	0.77
United Kingdom	real rate	0.39	0.39
	G-7 average rate	0.82	0.75
Canada	real rate	0.33	0.26
	G-7 average rate	0.88	0.55
1973–80			
United States	real rate	0.24	0.22
	G-7 average rate	0.22	0.19
Japan	real rate	0.14	0.19
	G-7 average rate	0.24	0.20
Germany	real rate	0.77	0.76
	G-7 average rate	0.21	0.17
France	real rate	0.31	0.29
	G-7 average rate	0.21	0.18
Italy	real rate	0.30	0.25
	G-7 average rate	0.22	0.19
United Kingdom	real rate	0.33	0.32
	G-7 average rate	0.21	0.18
Canada	real rate	0.32	0.36
	G-7 average rate	0.21	0.18
1981–91			
United States	real rate	0.17	0.11
	G-7 average rate	0.36	0.20
Japan	real rate	0.60	0.42
	G-7 average rate	0.19	0.10
Germany	real rate	0.38	0.45
	G-7 average rate	0.20	0.10

Table 16. (*cont.*)

		Sargan–Bhargava Test	
		H_0: random walk (1)	H_0: random walk with drift (2)
France	real rate	0.21	0.50
	G-7 average rate	0.21	0.11
Italy	real rate	0.42	0.34
	G-7 average rate	0.21	0.18
United Kingdom	real rate	0.26	0.14
	G-7 average rate	0.23	0.12
Canada	real rate	0.26	0.21
	G-7 average rate	0.22	0.11

Augmented Dickey–Fuller Test (ADF)

Lag	τ_τ (3)	τ_μ (4)	τ (5)	φ_3 (6)	φ_1 (7)
4	−0.68	−1.16	−0.14	0.66	0.69
4	−1.12	−1.25	−0.94	0.76	0.97
3	−2.16	−2.18	−1.20	2.34	2.69
4	−2.19	−2.20	−0.60	2.48	2.48
4	−1.97	−1.82	−1.31	1.94	1.84
4	−2.40	−2.30	−0.63	2.90	2.71
4	−1.00	−1.30	−1.00	0.84	0.93
4	−2.66	−2.37	−0.69	3.63	2.92
4	−2.69	−2.51	−1.46	3.62	3.39
4	−2.31	−2.33	−0.50	2.69	2.74
3	−2.29	−2.22	−1.05	2.69	2.63
4	−2.09	−2.09	−0.70	2.20	2.28
3	−3.75	−3.88	−4.01	7.33	7.76
4	−2.11	−1.95	−2.14	2.38	2.22
4	−1.94	−1.79	−2.56	2.70	4.01
2	−2.97	−2.68	−2.66	4.58	3.60
3	−5.72	−5.44	−0.17	16.40	14.94
4	−2.09	−1.81	−2.01	2.27	1.98

Table 16. (*cont.*)

Augmented Dickey–Fuller Test (ADF)

Lag	τ_τ (3)	τ_μ (4)	τ (5)	φ_3 (6)	φ_1 (7)
3	−4.72	−3.47	−2.54	11.74	6.02
4	−2.06	−1.79	−1.99	2.21	1.89
4	−1.62	−1.20	−0.98	1.37	0.78
3	−3.76	−3.12	−3.28	7.15	5.15
2	−2.96	−2.86	−2.55	4.45	4.12
4	−2.10	−1.96	−2.22	2.39	2.38
2	−2.66	−1.66	−1.63	3.58	1.47
4	−2.04	−1.72	−1.95	2.15	1.82
4	−2.74	−0.98	−0.73	3.83	0.58
4	−3.02	−2.79	−0.03	5.28	3.94
3	−3.77	−2.00	−0.67	7.26	2.08
3	−3.84	−1.90	−0.18	7.95	1.82
4	−2.81	−2.67	−0.15	4.20	3.60
3	−3.99	−1.77	−0.28	8.33	1.58
4	−2.33	−3.27	−1.10	5.63	7.45
3	−3.97	−1.68	−0.29	8.41	1.42
3	−3.21	−2.80	−0.45	5.46	3.91
3	−3.88	−1.72	−0.21	8.15	1.48
3	−2.54	−1.86	−0.32	3.40	1.80
3	−4.17	−1.84	−0.25	9.51	1.69
3	−2.49	−2.67	−0.21	3.94	3.68
3	−4.13	−1.80	−0.24	9.05	1.63

Note: Quarterly data. The critical values of the Sargan–Bhargava test are tabulated in J. D. Sargan and A. Bhargava, 'Testing Residuals from Least Squares Regression for Being Generated by the Gaussian Random Walk', *Econometrica* (1983), no. 51, those of the τ test in W. A. Fuller, *Introduction to Statistical Time Series* (New York: Wiley, 1976), table 8.5.2, and those of the φ_1, and φ_3 tests in D. A. Dickey and W. A. Fuller, 'Likelihood Ratio Statistics for Autoregressive Time Series with a Unit Root', *Econometrica* (1981), no. 49, 1057–77.

(1) Test of hypothesis $\rho = 1$ in the unrestricted model

$$Y_t = \mu + \rho Y_{t-1} + e_t, \qquad |\rho| < 1.$$

(2) Test of hypothesis $\rho = 1$ in the unrestricted model

$$Y_t - bt = \mu + \rho[Y_{t-1} - b(t-1)] + e_t, \qquad |\rho| < 1.$$

(3) Test of hypothesis $\rho = 1$ in the unrestricted model

$$Y_t = \alpha_0 + \rho Y_{t-1} + \alpha_1 \Delta y_{t-1} + \ldots + \alpha_n \Delta y_{t-n} + \beta(t - T/2) + e_t.$$

Table 16. (*cont.*)

---

(4) Test of hypothesis $\rho = 1$ in the unrestricted model

$$Y_t = \alpha_0 + \rho Y_{t-1} + \alpha_1 \Delta y_{t-1} + \ldots + \alpha_n \Delta y_{t-n} + e_t.$$

(5) Test of hypothesis $\rho = 1$ in the unrestricted model

$$Y_t = \rho Y_{t-1} + \alpha_1 \Delta y_{t-1} + \ldots + \alpha_n \Delta y_{t-n} + e_t.$$

(6) Test of joint hypothesis $\beta = 0$ and $\rho = 1$ in the unrestricted model as per note (3).

(7) Test of joint hypothesis $\alpha_0 = 0$ and $\rho = 1$ in the unrestricted model as per note (4).

Table 17. Regressions and co-integration test of long-term real interest rates (quarterly figures)

	Coefficients		$\bar{R}^2$	CRDW	ADF	
	Constant	Average G-7 rate				Lags
1960–72						
United States	3.10	-0.73	0.17	0.63	-1.83	4
Germany	2.50	0.75	0.04	0.32	-1.58	4
France	0.45	0.57	0.02	0.38	-1.93	4
Italy	2.95	-0.08	-0.02	0.18	-1.34	4
UK	0.47	1.06	0.04	0.48	-2.82	4
Canada	4.88	-0.80	0.11	0.58	-2.06	4
1973–80						
United States	-0.11	1.07	0.73	0.12	-1.21	2
Japan	-0.82	1.88	0.25	0.16	-1.91	4
Germany	2.82	-0.01	-0.03	0.79	-5.48	3
France	-0.45	0.54	0.48	0.53	-4.81	3
Italy	-2.59	1.56	0.55	0.56	-1.57	4
UK	-1.25	0.55	0.02	0.35	-2.06	4
Canada	0.60	0.56	0.34	0.48	-2.25	4

1981–91						
United States	-0.48	2.45	0.28	0.19	4	-1.47
Japan	1.64	0.60	0.42	0.77	3	-2.77
Germany	4.40	0.10	-0.01	0.37	3	-3.34
France	5.15	-0.06	-0.02	0.21	3	-2.85
Italy	2.68	0.24	0.02	0.43	3	-2.17
UK	-1.19	1.18	0.48	0.52	4	-1.72
Canada	0.75	0.98	0.39	0.27	3	-2.26

Note: the critical values of the Durbin–Watson test of the residuals of the co-integrating regression are tabulated in Sargan and Bhargava, op. cit.; for the ADF test, see note to Table 16.

Table 18. Regressions and co-integration test of long-term real interest rates (quarterly figures)

	Coefficients		$\bar{R}^2$	CRDW	ADF	
	Constant	German rate			Lags	
1960–72						
Italy	-1.00	0.98	0.30	0.34	4	-1.91
France	3.39	0.30	0.08	0.44	4	-2.11
United States	3.20	-0.25	0.13	0.70	4	-1.72
1973–80						
Italy	-2.50	-0.21	-0.03	0.31	4	-1.22
France	1.27	-0.70	0.11	0.40	3	-3.26
United States	0.74	-0.43	-0.10	0.28	3	-3.64
1981–91						
Italy	0.81	0.61	0.16	0.53	3	-3.14
France	0.53	0.90	0.33	0.41	4	-2.91
United States	5.84	-0.12	-0.02	0.19	3	-1.11

Note: See note to Table 17.